Aquafun – First Step

Note

For reasons of clarity and simplicity this book has been written using the male form of address. However, this refers to both sexes.

Uwe Rheker

Aquafun

First Steps

Learning by Playing

Meyer & Meyer Sport

Original Title
Rheker, Uwe: Alle ins Wasser
Spielend schimmen – schwimmend spielen
Band 1: Spiel und Spaß für Anfänger
© Aachen: Meyer & Meyer, 2003
Translated by Isabel Schmallofsky

British Library Cataloguing in Publication Data
A catalogue record for this book is available from the British Library

Rheker, Uwe:
Aquafun – First Steps
Learning by Playing / Uwe Rheker.
Oxford: Meyer & Meyer Sport (UK) Ltd, 2004
ISBN 1-84126-080-0

© 2004 by Meyer & Meyer Sport (UK) Ltd.
Oxford, Aachen, Olsten (CH), Vienna, Quebec, New York
Adelaide, Auckland, Johannesburg, Budapest
Member of the World
Sports Publishers' Association
Printed and bound: FINIDIR, s. r. o., Český Těšín
E-mail: verlag@m-m-sports.com
www.m-m-sports.com

Contents

Contents

III   ELEMENTARY SWIMMING TECHNIQUES 201

3   Preliminary Considerations, Teaching Techniques in Swimming Instruction 201

4   Index 222

5   Photo and Illustration Credits .223

6   Literature 224

FOREWORD

Foreword

Water, as an element in which one can move, should be available to everybody. Water offers fun and games for toddlers, children, young people, adults and older people. Water is an element in which the handicapped[1]) and non-handicapped alike can move, and in which they can jointly gain new experiences. It is an element for people of various physical and intellectual abilities. Water permits many fundamental experiences not possible on land. Especially for non-swimmers and beginners, water offers exciting encounters and many learning experiences that open up a world of new motion.

The various experiences with different groups of people (toddlers, handicapped children and young people), as well as experiences gained during swimming lessons and training at school and in the club, are summarized in this book and give ideas for all the many and varied groups of beginners. Special emphasis is placed on swimming with the physically and intellectually handicapped, because water, as an element in which these people can move, enables people with various abilities to come together (cf., Chapter 1.3.4). My thanks go primarily to the *Stiftung Westfalen* (The Westphalia Foundation), which has supported the project "Swimming as a Sport for Promoting Integration".

A special word of thanks goes to the academic staff and students who contributed to the preparation of this publication with unequalled commitment.

Paderborn, February 2004

Uwe Rheker

[1] In this book, this term describes all types of handicaps, physical as well as intellectual.

Preface

The more playfully swimming is taught, the more enjoyable it is, and the more fun swimming is, the more often it will be done.

The experience is equally valid for the handicapped as well as for the non-handicapped. And what could be more obvious for author Uwe Rheker than to make this experience the starting point for his integrative pedagogical concept, particularly since his teaching method meets the main physical characteristic of water: hydrostatic buoyancy.

Water will bear all people, irrespective of their age, sex, psychophysical ability, physical or intellectual limitations or handicaps - that is if they go into the water to play and try out the limits of their physical mobility in this element. Starting from this integrative and all-embracing swimming concept, this book offers a practical guide for instructors and a considerable collection of swimming games and methodical and organizational aids.

The book also goes into a series of additional teaching aspects so that even experienced swimming coaches can be initiated and made more sensitive to their teaching methods. For this reason alone I hope this book finds its way into the hands of as many practitioners as possible.

Cologne, March 2004

Kurt Wilke

1 THE FUNDAMENTALS

"If you wish to drink pure water, go to the source."

(French proverb)

1 Introduction

In this chapter, we will look at a few basic points that should be borne in mind when taking beginners swimming. Firstly, we will look at why there is good value in the experience of movement, fun and sport in water and why this is so important. Water is an element in which we can experience something unique.

Swimming is marked by pedagogical considerations. Why does swimming have such a special place in our society? Thinking about this question leads us to answers that are important in learning to swim and the ability to swim for different groups in very different contexts. The examination of a few historical examples leads us to see various concepts of swimming instruction for beginners, because the many "schools of thought" on swimming can only be explained in a historical context.

The fact that swimming is suitable for quite different types of people, and at the same time it is a competitive sport as well, where the various pre-requisites do not have such an importance, is covered in Chapter 1.4, "Swimming as an Integrative Sport".

The problem of fear (Chapter 1.5), particularly for beginners, is a very important factor.

The chapter on motivation (1.6) covers not only the question of overcoming fear during swimming instruction, but also shows how learning can be made into a more positive experience.

The question of the best age at which to learn to swim (Chapter 1.7) is considered from various points of view – from swimming for babies to swimming for mature learners.

The questions 'Which technique should be used after having learned to swim?' and 'What arguments are there in favor of starting with one swimming style or another?', the arguments for and against any initial technique, with reference to the crawl, backstroke crawl and breast stroke are discussed in Chapter 1.8.

Games equipment and swimming aids are introduced in the following chapter (Chapter 1.9) and their uses are elaborated upon.

The chapter "Organizing Swimming Instruction" (Chapter 1.10) concerns itself with the general conditions and legal background of giving swimming instruction (Swimming Regulations etc.).

The chapter on "Forms of Organization" (Chapter 1.11) leads to the practical aspects of swimming instruction, showing how the content can be organized best in order to achieve the aims successfully.

1.1   Water – A Special Element

"There, where water comes to rest, the water lily can grow and bloom."

(Ottilie Maag)

Water is an element that gives us experiences that are possible nowhere else on earth.

The feeling of **weightlessness** is granted only to the very few who can afford a flight into space. In water we can remain suspended in three dimensions by using controlled breathing and without aids such as oxygen bottle or ventilator equipment. Divers using the appropriate equipment over a long period of time can experience this great feeling. Unfortunately the "normal swimmer" has to come to the surface again after a short time (30-60 seconds), but can move around relatively "weightlessly" or just drift on the surface, for example, by playing "dead". For this exercise, you lie calmly on your back in the water and let yourself drift, controlling the depth of the body in the water by adjusting the breathing.

For learners, water is often an alien element that causes fear (cf., Chapter 1.5).

Since the beginning of man's existence, every human has had a positive attitude to water. For babies it is a **familiar element** that often causes pleasure and positive experiences, because, up until birth, the embryo moves around the womb inside the amniotic sac, swimming and "diving" in the element of water. For this reason the newborn baby feels very much at home in water and loves bath time.

In the first months of a baby's life, many activities are still determined by reflex actions. For example, the gripping reflex, effected by touching the palm of the hand, enables the baby to hold firmly onto its parent. Some protective reflexes even enable the baby to learn swimming and diving at an early stage. When water enters the breathing passages, the throat reflexively closes preventing water entering the upper extremities of the lungs, which we know as "swallowing water". Many swimming courses for babies make use of this reflex action and start teaching them to swim only months after being born (cf., Chapter 1.7).

As we know, water can be liquid, solid and gaseous. It can separate itself from other matter or dissolve others such as salt or sugar.

Water has special **characteristics**:

- Density (Viscosity)
- Pressure
- Resistance
- Buoyancy
- Conductivity of Heat
- Humidity

The higher **density of water** (compared to air and its molecular structure) has an effect on any body that is submersed in it. Even standing chest high in water makes breathing difficult for humans, as they have to inhale against the pressure that water exerts on their rib cage. Even gentle activities in water contribute to the strengthening of the breathing muscles. At the same time, exhaling becomes easier. For this reason spending time chest high in water, possibly in conjunction with doing water gymnastics, games or swimming different strokes, is particularly suitable for those with asthma problems.

Water pressure also promotes the circulation of blood in the veins back to the heart. It also eases the pressure on the legs of those people suffering from varicose veins. Because of this increased flow of venous blood, water pressure makes the heart pump greater quantities of blood around the body. This is compensated for by the frequent passing of urine. For this reason, children should be reminded to go to the toilet after long periods in the water.

In water we experience a noticeable **resistance** when moving. We are unable to move as quickly or as easily as on land. Particularly rapid movements are slowed down by the resistance of the water. This phenomenon has a beneficial effect on hyperactive and restless children as their activities are slowed down by the resistance of the water. Simultaneously, they use more strength and thus tire more quickly, and this can lead to a general "calming" effect.

For some forms of disability, the resistance caused by the water can also have other positive effects. In people suffering from spastic athetosis, the superfluous, reflex-like movements are inhibited and calmer movements become apparent.

However, water resistance not only "hinders" human movement, it can also act additionally as a means of moving the body forward when using the hands or feet to walk or run in water. Rapid movements in water require more effort than on land, as greater resistance has to be overcome. On the other hand, slow movements, that don't require much effort, are possible and are often easier than on dry land. A lot less strength is required to counter gravity in water. It is thus easier to swing one's arms backwards and forwards in water than on land.

Buoyancy is responsible for this phenomenon. Any body immersed in water experiences buoyancy (according to the Archimedes' Principle). Put simply this means that any body in water loses as much weight as it displaces water. This buoyancy effect counters gravity and is as great as the quantity of water it displaces. Buoyancy takes the load off the human body, especially the joints. For this reason, people, even with damaged joints, are still able to do water gymnastics, swimming and games in water, long after the same exercises on land wouldn't be advisable any more.

Water has a higher **conductivity of warmth** than air (about 25 times greater). For this reason we feel the temperature in water more intensely. Even relatively warm water (28-30°C) causes the body to cool down when in water for longer periods. By contrast, an air temperature of 28°C is still considered to be warm even after several hours. The cooling effect of water on small children is even greater, as they have a larger body-surface than adults compared to the size and weight of their bodies. For this reason care must be taken with children and people with various forms of disability (e.g. children with muscular dystrophy or spastic paralysis), by warming their bodies under a warm shower to prevent cooling off.

We experience **humidity** in different ways. Having a shower or jumping into cool water can thus be refreshing. However, for nervous people, a spray of water or wet hair can be an unpleasant experience.

For humans, animals and plants, water is the **elixir of life**. All living beings depend on water; only 'camels' can go without water for long periods. After a longer period of physical effort such as a marathon, for example, or a hot summer's day, a gulp of cool water gets you going again.

Water can be refreshing. If a long, exhausting walk in the mountains leads us to a clear spring, this cool, potable water is not only physically refreshing but it is also a sign of something natural and exhilarating for the whole person. We experience this refreshing element if we can enjoy it with our whole body, for example, by jumping into a lake.

In such situations, it becomes clear how important clean water is for all living beings and how important it is to protect the environment. But there are only a few rivers or lakes left that we can swim in without any danger to our health. For this reason, being able to swim in **open water**, which was possible almost everywhere 40 years ago, is a very valuable experience. Lately, being allowed to swim or dive in a clear mountain lake has become a rare thing to experience nature. Swimming in the sea, with its waves and breakers, adds a new dimension to our experiences with water. Water can show its great strength, which we can look at in awe when watching the waves breaking, but it also has the potential for destruction – particularly evident in storm tides or floods.

But the rushing sound of the sea or the splashing of a little stream can also be **restful**. For example there is music to relax to with the rushing tide or a trickling stream as a basic theme.

Relaxation exercises can also be carried out very easily in water. For example, it is possible to lie relaxed on the water with or without the support of floating aids such as paddle-boards, pull-buoys or aqua-jogging vests after the exertion of a swim or water gymnastics. Even treading cold water in a basin, as per Kneipp's methods, is good for the health.

Water is not only the elixir of life and the element from which all life comes, it is also an **unknown, alien environment** for us. We cannot breathe under water and stay submerged for long periods without a lot of preparation and the necessary equipment (diving equipment). We can see plants and animals there, which do not exist on land. We can admire the many varieties of colorful tropical fish, but also remain aware of the danger of stingrays, octopuses and sharks.

Water is thus, in many ways, a special element, which holds many experiences in store for us.

1.2   The Importance of Swimming

"Do good to thy body, that thy soul will want to dwell therein."

(Teresa of Avila)

Swimming occupies a position of special importance in our society. It can be carried out for a variety of reasons. Some people go swimming regularly in order to do something for their health. Others do it in order to keep up social contacts etc. How sport can be interpreted, and here in particular swimming, has already been extensively covered in the didactic sport literature (cf., Kurz, 1990; Kurz & Volck, 1977; Scherler, 1981; Volck, 1982 et al). These arguments will not be repeated here. However, we will go through the varied aspects of why swimming is important for us.

Discarding a more technique-related interpretation of the concept of swimming, in which it was understood that swimming was a movement in a straight line in a standard sized pool in one of the four Olympic techniques, opens up a variety of perspectives. Swimming constitutes various ways of moving in, on and under water (cf., Scherler, 1981). However, a broader interpretation gives an individual approach to water as a place for many types of sensory experience.

For this reason the different interpretations that follow are to be understood as a framework, within which the individual, whether he be a beginner swimmer an advanced swimmer, someone playing water polo or a diver etc., can try out various ways in which he can move and play. In this way a subjective process of analysis of the element "water" (Hildebrandt, 1993, 1999) is introduced, giving a new environment to move in, and which opens up the different ways one can learn, play and move in, on, and under water.

1.2.1   Having Fun

In the many surveys carried out with young people concerning their preferred sport, the special importance of swimming is highlighted. According to a study by Brettschneider & Bräutigam (1990), swimming is the sport most frequently carried out by young, non-handicapped people in various environments – with the family, as a leisure pursuit or in a clique with friends of the same age (1990: 58-62). Similar studies by Blücher (1966), Sack (1985) et al., show the same results. The outstanding importance of swimming for handicapped, young people is illustrated in the study by Brettschneider & Rheker (1966), commissioned by the Ministry of Education and Cultural Affairs in the State of North Rhine-Westphalia.

Swimming is a clear favorite over other types of sports with handicapped children and teenagers. This is so for sporting activities of those both at active club level and as a leisure activity, as well as sports that they would like to take part in (cf., Brettschneider & Rheker, 1966: 45-49; Rheker, 1996c: 62-76).

For handicapped and non-handicapped children and teenagers, the dominant motive for taking part in sport is *to have fun* (cf., Brettschneider & Bräutigam, 1990: 54; Brettschneider & Rheker, 1966: 41ff., Rheker, 1996b: 103). This first, main motive for young non-handicapped people is followed by the complex of *health, fitness and the body.*

By contrast, the second, main motive for handicapped children and teenagers is centered on social experience (cf., Rheker, 1996c: 59). The increasing importance of fun is made clear in the "swimming pool" culture. Old swimming pools, in which it is only possible to swim in a straight line, have decreasing numbers of visitors. The "fun and experience" pools, on the other hand, are much in demand.

1.2.2   Health

Most people, who join a sports club or go swimming in their spare time, do so in order "to do something for their health". *Health, fitness and relaxation* in swimming, playing and moving in water are just as important as *having fun* (Brettschneider & Bräutigam, 1990). Here the term health is related not only to the physical side of personal well being. Following the definition of the World Health Organisation (WHO), health includes not only organic-physical and psychological aspects, but also mental and social aspects. A person's social environment also contributes to his general well being and, hence, to his health.

The **organic-physical** dimension of health relates primarily to the cardiovascular, respiratory and metabolic as well as to the supportive and motor apparatus of the body. Here, deliberately doing a "sports activity" creates a balance to counter the monotonous strain of one's job. Alternatively, one can simply and deliberately do something for one's own physical fitness. In this way, stamina-related exertion such as running, swimming or cycling can improve cardiovascular performance, breathing and the metabolism, so that everyday strains can be coped with better. One feels fit and capable of more or can actively avoid the onset of a heart attack (cf., also Prevention/Rehabilitation Chapter 1.2.14). On the other hand, specific training can increase muscle performance for strength, speed and acceleration and improve the posture or even simply aim at it in order to change the physical appearance (cf., the ideal of beauty in a bodybuilder). This health-related dimension of doing sport often has to do with concepts such as:

- getting rid of a paunch or the extra pounds put on in winter.
- cutting a good figure.
- compensating for lack of movement.
- satisfying an urge for movement.
- reacting to inner-tension etc.

The psychological side of the concept of health, which is very closely connected with the previous views, can be defined by using terms of emotional states such as well being, freedom from fear, a relaxed feeling, a sense of security and fun. At the same time, the fun and pleasure experienced, when playing around in water and swimming, can lead to harmony and a reduction of inner-tension. This psycho-physical adjustment can be achieved specifically through relaxation training and water gymnastics. Time spent moving about in water improves the health generally and leads to a more intensive awareness of the body. However, swimming can also lead to health-related risks. Chilling and physical strain, through to non-swimmers drowning in deep or unfamiliar water, are only a few of these risk factors.

1.2.3   Physical Experience

Swimming makes it possible for us to experience certain special **physical effects**. Water, with its specific characteristics of density, pressure, buoyancy and its ability to conduct warmth, opens up a particular awareness of the body to the swimmer.

Even very small children can learn things when starting to swim as a baby, and these develop and intensify their understanding of their body. For example, the child learns the difference between up and down when floating in the water on its stomach or its back. Through direct contact of the skin with water, it learns to feel the difference between warm and cold. While playing with various toys, e.g., balls, ducks, little boats, snorkels and water masks, swimming-boards etc., children learn how to handle and use them in water. Doing this they can develop their perceptive faculties so that they can "understand" the environment better. Even tiny infants are able to develop elementary movement motions and deliberately move towards somebody else in the water, where, on dry land they would still find it impossible to make forward movements of this kind. Movement in water gives us all new spatial experiences, which we could not, in most cases, normally perform on land. As a result, people can float in the water, move in three dimensions, carry out rolling movements in any axis they wish, make sideways somersault movements, make vertical screw-like movements, do backward or forward head-over rolling movements, or even combined movements like the double screw-roll. The physical strain when swimming, playing and training in the water is experienced very directly - not only just tiredness, but also recovery and relaxation; all can be felt intensively by the body.

1.2.4   Special Perception

When swimming, playing or diving in and under water, our sense of perception is "unique". For example, our vision without swimming goggles is very blurry, whereas with them we can see objects better and clearer. Our hearing also changes under water. We can perceive noises and sounds more directly and over greater distances. It's a fun thing to recognize songs being sung under water - no easy task. Voices are certainly only comprehensible with difficulty or hardly at all. For this reason divers have developed a sign language for diving, which opens up a new way of communication.

Our tactile perception of the environment when in water is more direct than on land. We can feel the warmth or coldness of the water more intensively. When gliding through water we perceive the water around us as a frontal or a whirlpool-like resistance or can enjoy, for example, moving dolphin-like through the water. We get a pleasant feeling after a successful dive from a three-meter springboard without splashing. On the other hand, a belly-flop into the water from a low height, with a big splash of the body not in the right position, can cause a very unpleasant sensation.

1.2.5 Physical Experience

Water makes specific physical experiences possible. Through movement, humans can relate to their physical and social environment and come to terms with it. Through such "material experiences" (Scherler, 1975), children become acquainted with things and objects in the environment. By comparing them with each other they can categorize them. By experimenting with them and handling them, the child's motor system learns to use or accommodate them. As the child becomes more mobile, it adapts itself more to the areas of its environment that open up to it e.g., from crawling and walking through to running, climbing, and jumping over obstacles etc.

Only by being in water do we experience its special characteristics - and, indeed, right up close. Water is wet and through its increased ability to conduct warmth and coldness we feel these more directly and clearly. Water gives way, but also creates resistance. Water is soft, but can also be relatively hard, e.g., when we dive into it on our backs. We experience the buoyancy it exerts on parts of our bodies. But even various objects used for playing, diving and training behave differently in water. Thus balls rise to the surface, while an underwater ball, filled with saltwater, sinks.

1.2.6 Social Experience

Swimming is a sport that allows us to experience special social aspects. Apart from reasons of health, another reason for joining a sports club or carrying out sports activities in leisure time lies in the search for social contact and communication (Kurz, 1990: 99; Rheker, 1996c: 59). By playing sport or just playing with others it is easier for some to be able to make contact with other people, to get into conversation with them or to get together and do things when the sports session is over. Sport, and particularly games, make communication and social interaction easier. From beginners swimming to leisure sports, or popular sporting activities, up to competitive sports, swimming offers many opportunities for social experience.

Games and exercises in beginners swimming are chosen mostly so that everybody can take part and gain experience of various movements, which eventually lead to confidence in swimming. Singing games or games carried out in a circle, communicative and interactive games, little ball games or games using equipment are suitable for such experiences. When getting started in other sports such as soccer, some participants may have previous experience (and others none). In swimming, everyone starts mostly at the same level of ability. With swimming and other games in water, the differences between old and young, handicapped and non-handicapped are not so great, so everyone can play together. For this reason, social motives for handicapped children and young people wanting to get involved in swimming have a special significance (cf., Rheker, 1996b: 103).

In swimming lessons at school, the integration of not-so-capable pupils and other outsiders often works better than in other lessons by using interactive games, joint movement exercises with music or new subjects, such as diving and life-saving swimming. Particularly, elements of life-saving swimming can promote the children's sense of social responsibility and, in turn, achieve the social learning goals of the swimming instruction. Besides special sessions of family sports, it is one of the few opportunities for parents or grandparents to enjoy sport together with their little or older children. This applies equally to families with handicapped children as well as those with non-handicapped children. For this reason swimming is an ideal "integrative" sport (cf., Chapter 1.4).

1.2.7   Independence

Apart from learning to walk, the experience of learning to swim on one's own is a very important stage in the development of the personality of a young person. By being able to swim, a person has "swum himself free", so to speak, from adult supervision and a new habitat can now be explored. It is now possible to take part in the games and activities of the "swimmers" in the big pool, to be able to jump into the 'deep end' and to dive, and move in three dimensions etc. Now that you are confident enough to try more things, this independence means more self-confidence and self-assurance. Fear of drowning has been overcome. It is now even possible to assume responsibility for others by doing a life-saving course. The variety of ways of moving around, in and under water, with and without aids, results in not only experiencing the movements, but also in the development of creativity, new ideas, and self-realization through the medium of games.

1.2.8   Playing Games

Using the term 'play', to start with, we refer to an activity solely done for our own pleasure, and which is quite separate from work or anything serious. In soccer or water polo, however, we can hardly detect anything of the original meaning of the term 'play'. The pure joy of playing is certainly evident in less competitive or success-oriented games. According to Lange, 'play' is defined as the unrestrained activity with elements and objects of reality; that is to say the "manipulation" of such elements and objects in order to overcome their apparent limitations and restrictive effect, thereby shaping and altering circumstances (1977: 16). This can be demonstrated using the example of the game of water polo. In this game, the players can, within the rules, "manipulate" the ball, space, time and their opponents i.e., to work with them to create and change game situations by gaining control of the ball, take it forward and shoot at goal, or to help fellow team-members to block or outplay their opponents. They can also structure the play tactically (e.g., by swimming to become unmarked, by breaking away from their opponents, by dribbling around or by outnumbering the opposition etc.,) or just play for time. Of course, all this takes place in the major sports games within the prescribed rules. There is no room to manipulate or break the rules in the official competitive version of water polo, but it probably goes on in friendly games. With beginner swimmers, particularly, there are many opportunities to play using rules and to vary simple games or to "invent" new ones. When tasked, children can be very inventive in thinking up new game ideas themselves. Therefore, particularly during children's swimming lessons, room should be created for free play or for children to have the opportunity to join in and be creative in the development of ideas for games.

1.2.9   Performance and Competition

Swimming can also be carried out with the perspective of performance and optimizing performance. When children are learning to swim and, for the first time, can swim a width of a swimming pool, this is an achievement they can be proud of. Through systematic training, their performance can be deliberately stepped up. Increasing performance in swimming therefore means acquiring the physical (i.e., organic-physical and motor) condition necessary to be able to cover a given length using a particular stroke in as short a time as possible (cf., Lange: 1977, 14).

This can be achieved

* by improving technique, as well as
* by improving basic physical ability: stamina, strength, speed, and the complex of associated characteristics of speed endurance, muscular power and acceleration.

The motivation to do something for one's fitness is more marked in competitive swimming than in leisure and popular sports. But even in their leisure time many people also go swimming with the object of maintaining their health in order to keep fit or to regain fitness. For many people, who like swimming and playing in water, performance has a special importance, even when this interpretation is not at the top of their list.

1.2.10   Reaching New Heights

Improving performance leaves the question open whether the yardstick of the competition or the record is the reference point of one's own performance. Often, at least in competitive sport, the interpretation of improving performance is linked to breaking records. In this way, a particular individual performance – a "personal swimming time" – is noted as a standard or a quality that can be compared with that of others. It is then possible to judge whether this was a good or a poor time. All this starts with friends, at school and continues to national and international levels.

1.2.11   Leisure Activities - Leisure Sports

Swimming, with its variety of movements, opens up just as many sporting as well as leisure-oriented activities:

* swimming as an ideal stamina sport.
* swimming as a sprint sport (swimming fast over short distances).
* a variety of movements:
    – from the four main competition techniques to the thousands of creative or individual movement techniques.
* the method of entering the water can be varied:
    – from a simple entry feet first through to the traditional dive in and up to springboard diving and high-diving.

- ways of entering the water can be performed ranging from being accompanied by music up to springboard diving and synchronized swimming.
- playing games in water:
  - from simple swimming and catching games, games using little balls through to larger ball games such as water polo, water soccer, water basketball, water rugby, water volleyball, water biathlons or underwater ball games, snorkeling and diving.
- health-oriented games performed in water:
  - water gymnastics, gymnastics for the back and spine, aqua-jogging etc.

1.2.12   The Aesthetics and Creative Aspects of Swimming

In sport, when considered against this interpretation, it's all about the special way in which movements are carried out and how the motions and the moving body appears. The emphasis is not on measurable criteria such as those in javelin throwing or the long-jump. Nor is it about results such as scoring five or six goals. Rather, it is about the appreciation of the total movement. In swimming, this is particularly the case in springboard and high-diving and artistic and synchronized swimming, as well as during "aesthetic swimming", where attention is paid to one's own swimming style. In my opinion, the development of one's own creativity and spontaneity, and one's imagination, finding out the different ways in which one can move in water, are also included in this interpretation.

These objectives can be achieved during swimming lessons by simple movement exercises, in which the pupils, for example:

- are allowed to develop their own creative movements in the water.
- are able to develop their own movements accompanied by music – alone or in groups.
- are able to try out creative and funny jumps into the water etc., – alone or in groups.

Movement exercises like these not only have the advantage that people discover swimming and games in all their variations in the water; it is also fun for school pupils and older people to discover new movements and games and to broaden and give them new variations of their movements.

1.2.13 Adventure, Risk and Tension

In many types of sports and many sporting situations, tension is created by the uncertain outcome of the situation. In particular, games between two opponents of equal strength are tense where the result of the competition is not certain for a long time. This tension can increase to become a great inner tension and turn out to be an adventurous experience. This is where situations occur that ought to be overcome or where the situation conceals a subjective risk (danger):

* swimming for the first time out of depth, in the open sea or in breakers.
* putting one's head under water for the first time, diving lessons, diving with equipment in open water, or diving in a current or at night.
* playing underwater polo or rugby.

The increasing importance of "adventure games" in the swimming pool, especially in adventure swimming pools, underlines the significance of this concept. Swimming pools gain in attractiveness when they are fitted with interesting equipment and offer a variety of unusual sorts of amusements such as waterslides, wobbling bridges, octopuses, overhead cable slides, bathtub races or water trampolines etc.

1.2.14 Prevention/Rehabilitation

Sport, in the sense of 'prevention' or 'rehabilitation', has a special significance not only present in sports with the handicapped. 'Prevention' is closely related to health, fitness and relaxation. This is because consciously doing a sports activity can help prevent complaints caused by lack of exercise such as the danger of a heart attack, fatty liver, overweight etc. In the same way, doing gymnastics and swimming, especially doing the backstroke, can contribute towards healing bad posture and reduce and compensate for a weak posture.

We first come in contact with sport as a rehabilitating measure after such an injury, for example:

1. Rehabilitation after an injury (e.g., a broken leg); sport and special gymnastics to restore physical performance (strengthening of the atrophied muscles, therapy to mobilize a "plastered" leg).

2. Sport as a therapy after a heart attack and then as a preventive measure (against a further attack) doing aerobic sport.

3. Sport as a form of rehabilitation for a congenital or physical handicap contracted later e.g., paraplegic injuries after an accident. Sport begins here already in the clinic with the following objectives:
   - Mobilization of motor abilities with the aid of suitable mobility exercises.
   - Training the non-injured muscles (e.g., through power training), to compensate for the lost abilities.
   - Improvement of the vegetative adaptive ability through a variety of physical exercises, targeting cardiopulmonary training (cf., Kosel, 1981).
   - Social integration through joint sports activities in a group.

In particular, swimming, with its variety of movements, offers extensive opportunities also for people, who, for example, cannot take part in other sports activities on land because of injured joints. Water gymnastics, aqua-jogging and aqua-fitness training offer interesting forms of movements, which achieve the objective of prevention and rehabilitation.

1.2.15   A Door to the World of Water Sports

Being able to swim is the basis for many other sporting activities, which can be carried out in, under or on the water. The door to the world of such water sports as sailing, surfing, underwater diving, rowing, canoeing, kayaking, surfing, water-skiing or diving into the water inter alia, are only open to people when they can swim. Many new sports and leisure activities are thus open to the swimmer.

1.2.16   Swimming Can Save Lives

Swimming can contribute to saving human lives in many ways:

- As soon as they have learned to swim, beginners are able to avoid drowning, should they get into deep water by accident, and save themselves by swimming to safety.

- By learning life-saving techniques, a person is able to save someone who has got into difficulties. Generally, life-saving societies, lifeguards and other organizations have set themselves the goal of transferring this social responsibility to as many people as possible.
- Regular swimming is regarded as an ideal form of health-promoting sport. Proper swimming and mobility training in water, such as water gymnastics, aqua-jogging etc., are an excellent prophylaxis for the prevention of so-called "civilization diseases" such as heart attacks, overweight etc and they contribute to the ability to "save one's own life" – that is to lead a healthy life.

1.3   The Concept of Swimming for Beginners

"Intelligence is quickness to apprehend as distinct from ability, which is capacity to act wisely on the thing apprehended".

(A N Whitehead, 1939 – Dialogues)

1.3.1   Historical Survey

Even up to the modern age of today there were several methods of swimming instruction, which can only be understood in an historical background, so let's look at a few methods commonly used in the past.

The Dry Swimming Method
The dry swimming method was based on a more mechanistic understanding of swimming. It was presumed that anybody who could master the swimming movements could swim. For this reason the learning of swimming techniques (breaststroke) was emphasized by practicing it, first of all, on dry land. This was carried out partly on swimming "horses" or other land-based apparatus (cf., Wilke, 1992: 32-17).

Advocates of this swimming method are: D'arcy, Kluge, Euler and Auerbach among others.

The Counting Method

The method, by which swimming movements were divided up into numbers and then practiced according to this numbering, can be ascribed to General Von Pfuel (1809). The swimming instructor, pool supervisor or the army drillmaster stood at the side of the swimming pool and counted out loud "1,2,3" etc. The students had to carry out these movements in time with the numbers being called out. This clear, structured and simple method – the swimming instructor only had to count to "3" – was used for a very long time.

1.3.2   Kurt Wiessner's Swimming Methods for Beginners

Following Gaulhofer & Streicher (1922) and "natural gymnastics", which turned away from the drill method towards more natural movements, Kurt Wiessner (1925) wrote his handbook for swimming "Instruction in Natural Swimming". He saw psychological reasons and a lack of familiarity with water as the main arguments for not being able to swim. For this reason, at the beginning of his training concept, he included many exercises on becoming familiar with water. As Wiessner deliberately did without buoyancy aids, he was considered **the** protagonist of swimming instruction without aids. His methodical approach was as follows:

The first activities are games and exercises to get the pupils used to water:

- putting the head under water.
- floating in the water.
- floating freely.
- gliding along on top of the water.

These basic exercises are followed by exercises designed to teach swimming techniques. In contrast to the conventional techniques used to teach swimming, which lead to learning the breaststroke techniques to start with, Wiessner recommends doing both breaststroke and crawl exercises. Here he refrains from breaking the movements up into a sequence and does not use the number method. Arm and leg movements are practiced as a whole. These should be done boldly and should be practiced from the beginning in the water (cf., Wilke, 1979: 18). He introduces the techniques of the kick for the breaststroke or the crawl:

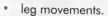

- leg movements.
- arm movements.
- coordination (arms and legs working together).
- breathing.
- complete movements (total coordination of limbs with breathing).

All "modern methods" of swimming for beginners are based on this idea.

1.3.3   Modern Methods

Of the many methodical concepts of swimming for beginners, the two that are regarded as the basic ones, pointing the way ahead, are introduced here. In former East Germany, the publication of Gerhard Lewin's work "Schwimmen mit kleinen Leuten" (Swimming with the little ones) (1967) was a varied and methodically well prepared specialist work. This has now appeared in a revised and lengthened form (cf., Lewin: 1994). An equally successful and fundamental work on swimming for beginners was published by Kurt Wilke (1979, 1992).

Swimming for Beginners According to Lewin
Lewin divides swimming instruction for beginners into three parts according to the basic considerations:

- exercises in shoulder-height water.
- exercises in water, deep enough to swim.
- the improvement and full use of basic swimming skills.

Each of these modules contains the following basic skills: underwater diving, jumping in and diving, gliding, moving in water and conscious breathing. In the first module the learner approaches these interim goals with the idea of "making friends with water, that only reaches up to my shoulders", using the following steps:

Underwater Diving	1. Immersing the face fully in the water. 2. Putting the head completely under the water. 3. Covering a short distance under chest-height water.
Jumping into the water	1. Jumping up and down in waist to chest-high water. 2. Jumping down into chest-high water. 3. Jumping into neck-deep water.
Gliding	1. Experiencing static buoyancy: • Keeping the balance while floating on one's stomach. • Keeping the balance while floating on one's back. • Keeping the balance while floating in a squatting position. 2. Experiencing dynamic buoyancy: • Gliding on the surface of the water on the back and the stomach (with support). • Pushing off from the side of the pool and gliding across the water on the back and the stomach.
Moving in the water	1. Recognizing and making use of the water resistance: (Walking forwards and backwards in waist-high to chest-high water with and without using the arms. 2. Introduction to kicking the legs. • on the back. • on the stomach.
Breathing in water.	1. Deep, conscious breathing out into the water. 2. Regular inhaling above the water and exhaling into the water 3. Rhythmical inhaling above the water and exhaling into the water 10 times.

Figure 3: *Swimming for Beginners according to Lewin (Lewin, 1994: 52-53)*

The same basic skills are developed further in the following teaching modules until they can be carried out in water deep enough to swim in. The arm and leg movements for the backstroke, the crawl and the breaststroke are practiced using the techniques required to do alternate arm and leg movements.

Swimming for Beginners According to Kurt Wilke

In "Swimming for Beginners", Kurt Wilke has written a very varied and comprehensive book. After a chapter on basic knowledge, (history, water as a medium, the health aspects of swimming, fear), he introduces the methodology of swimming for beginners; getting used to water, overcoming water, and the breaststroke.

He then writes about other authors who prefer the use of buoyancy aids (Silvia, Bauermeister, Hetz). The following topics are also covered; swimming in various groups (babies, parents-and-babies, pre-schoolers, adults, the handicapped and gymnastics for older learners) and various programs for advanced pupils.

The concept of swimming for beginners according to Wilke is divided into three main sections:

* getting used to water.
* coming to terms with water.
* learning the movements used in swimming (cf., Wilke, 1994: 38-45).

In **getting used to the water** Wilke has foregone the use of swimming aids. By means of games and exercises the pupils get used to water as a medium.

In **coming to terms with water** the pupils attempt to attain the following goals through a number of games and exercises:

* underwater diving
* jumping in and diving
* breathing

* floating and gliding
* the swimming position
* games in water

(cf., Wilke, 1994: 45-76)

1.3.4 Methodical Concepts in Swimming with the Handicapped

Lorenzen's Methods

In 1970, Hans Lorenzen wrote the first book about swimming for the handicapped entitled "Behinderte Schwimmen" (Swimming for the Handicapped). His concept is marked by a medical-therapeutic approach, and, among other things, is the basis of sport for the 'disabled', as the handicapped used to be called in those days, becoming known in society. Lorenzen's goals may be summarized as follows:

Purpose and Objectives

- Sport for the disabled as a means of healing (rehabilitation and prevention) contributes, physically and psychologically, to inner self-sufficiency, the maintenance of vigor and an increase in performance, thereby allowing them to gain more control over their lives.
- Sport for the disabled is for fit handicapped people.
- "The goal of these physical exercises, appropriate to the degree of disability, is to turn those in need of assistance into independent, helpful, employable people for their own advantage, and that of their families and the state." (cf., Lorenzen, 1961: 15).

As far as possible, the division into groups, according to Lorenzen's advice, should take place by placing similarly handicapped people together. In this way, the handicapped sportsmen and women stay amongst themselves. He does not envisage "non-disabled" and the handicapped participating in joint sport. The groups should also be similar in terms of age and sex.

The methods used to teach them to swim are divided into three main areas. Beginners:

- getting used to water and coming to terms with it.
- learning swimming techniques appropriate for the handicapped for leisure and competitive swimming: ordinary backstroke, breaststroke, sidestroke breast-crawl, backstroke crawl and butterfly.
- diving and water polo.

The interim goals for learning a particular swimming technique are set out here using the example of the technique for the ordinary backstroke.

• Those with a handicap in one arm	• Those with a leg handicap
• Floating on the back(with the support of the pool ladder)	• Playing water polo in a sitting position
• Exercises in diving for objects	• Letting the stumps of the legs float on the surface of the water while holding on to the pool ladder
• Floating on the back	• Floating, slowly letting go of the ladder support ('dead man')
• Doing a flying dive	• Floating and paddling with the arms
• Leg movements with the aid of support	• Doing a flying dive and gliding
• Doing a flying dive together with leg movements	• Moving the whole body including the arms

Figure 4: *Swimming for Beginners according to Lorenzen*

Innenmoser's Swimming Theories

Jürgen Innenmoser's book, "Schwimmspaß für Behinderte" (Swimming Fun for the Handicapped (1968)), must be seen as a basic and comprehensive work on swimming for the handicapped. Years of study on movement and experience in swimming instruction with all kinds of handicapped people, in various projects carried out at the Deutsche Sporthochschule (German College of Physical Education) in Cologne, bear witness to these statements. Following an introduction, which includes the reactions of handicapped pupils, he goes into the characteristics of water and its importance for the perception and movements of the handicapped. The significance of swimming, for people with various forms of handicaps, is dealt with in the next chapter. The chapters that follow are devoted to the methods used in swimming for beginners:

- General lesson aims.
- Structure of the swimming lessons for beginners and learning to swim for different age groups.
- Swimming techniques for the handicapped.
- Teaching tips.
- Organizational tips.

The methodical structure of swimming for beginners is of particular interest. Like Wilke (1979), he separates the themes of **getting used to the water** and **coming to terms with water**. In the section on **getting used to the water**, the aims are for the pupils to move actively around and experience water, both consciously and subconsciously, by doing the following:

- getting into the water, moving forward and being pulled around.
- playing with the instructor and – in a group – playing with objects while walking, running, hopping, jumping, pulling oneself along hand over hand with a rope, kicking or thrashing around.
- playing: blowing balls along, submerging, floating, surfacing.

(cf., Innenmoser, 1988: 71)

In the section on coming to terms with water, the pupils learn the following interim goals:

- Submerging
- Breathing
- Jumping in
- Surfacing
- Gliding through the water

These are done in sequences according to the degree of handicap:

The Phases of Coming to Terms with Water	1	2	3	4	5
Cerebrally damaged	Breathing	Jumping	Submerging	Surfacing	Gliding
Leg Handicapped	Surfacing	Gliding	Breathing	Diving	Jumping
Arm Handicapped	Gliding	Jumping	Diving	Breathing	Surfacing
Damaged Internal organs	Surfacing	Jumping	Diving	Breathing	Gliding
Sensory Handicapped	Gliding	Breathing	Diving	Surfacing	Jumping
Learning Handicapped	Jumping	Breathing	Gliding	Diving	Surfacing
Mentally Handicapped	Breathing	Surfacing	Diving	Jumping	Gliding
Maladjustment problems	Jumping	Gliding	Breathing	Diving	Surfacing

Figure 5: *Interim Learning Goals for Handicapped Swimming Learners* (Innenmoser, 1978: 78)

Possible combinations of exercises in individual teaching sessions:

1. Jumping in   +   diving
2. Jumping in   +   diving   +   floating
3. Breathing   +   diving
4. Floating   +   gliding
5. Diving   +   gliding
6. Jumping   +   breathing   +   diving

The Halliwick Method

In 1949, James McMillan, a former swimming instructor and hydraulics engineer, started arranging swimming courses at the London Halliwick School for Physically Handicapped Children together with a physiotherapist, a doctor and several voluntary helpers. For the mostly cerebrally, movement-impaired children, he developed a new method for swimming for the handicapped, which became known as the "Halliwick Method" (cf., Hasler-Rietmann, 1976: Weber-Witt, 1993).

This method did away with artificial buoyancy aids, even for severely handicapped children. By means of games, the children are meant to be totally stimulated by the water and their experiences in it, and develop a special awareness for their bodies. In this way, they would be placed in a position of being able to move around freely in the water without any aids. This is because swimming aids, such as water wings, give a false impression of the body's natural buoyancy and alter the conditions for the body's sense of balance. In any case, water is a medium where many handicapped people can do without the aids that they are dependent on on land. The Halliwick Method is based on a high ratio of helpers, where, first of all, each child has his own helper in the water.

A feeling of "absolute safety in the water" (Hasler-Rietmann, 1976: 256) is therefore one of the first goals in this method. The instruction also takes place in groups. The Halliwick Method is divided into 10 learning steps, which make instruction clear and easy to pass on. Only after these basic experiences have been mastered are the swimming techniques taught.

The 10-Point Program of the "Halliwick Method":

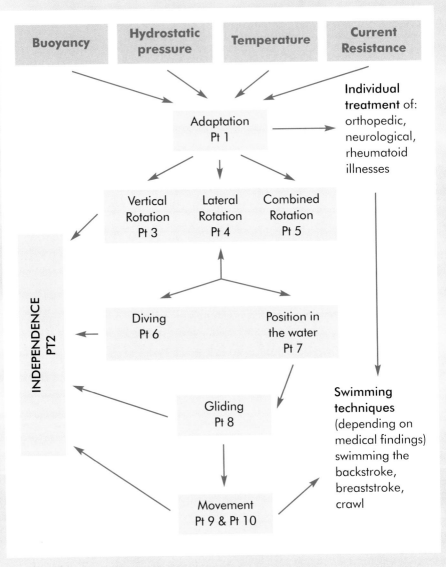

Figure 6: *The 10-Point Program of the Halliwick Method (Weber-Witt, 1993: 109)*

1. Adaptation (Psychological Adjustment)

Using playful activities, and with the aid of a helper, fear and uncertainty are broken down. At the same time, the child can be made familiar with the different conditions in the water and achieves self-confidence in its own abilities. Here the helper gives a feeling of absolute safety. The way of moving on land that the child has mastered is carried over into the water.

2. Independence

The support from the helper is reduced little by little. The child gradually becomes independent of the helper in order that the latter does not become a psychological "life belt".

3. Vertical Rotation

Vertical rotation means a rotation in the sagittal plane, in other words a movement from the vertical to the horizontal, from a standing position onto the stomach or the back. The child first learns to move, from a standing position onto the back and then back into a standing position again in the practice pool, with and, later, without help. Moving onto the stomach position is learnt in the same way. The head controls these movements. For this a certain degree of control of the head is demanded.

4. Lateral Rotation

Lateral rotation is a movement around the longitudinal axis of the body. Here the child learns to turn from lying on its back onto its stomach and back again. This movement is always begun using the head. The hands and arms can help to support this movement.

5. Combined Rotation

The combination, at the same time, of a lateral and a vertical rotation is a form of movement that one often does on land and in the water. In this swimming method it is called combined rotation. When, for example in the practice swimming pool, a pupil falls forward from a standing position and, while falling, turns over onto his back in order to keep his face free to breathe, he uses this combined rotation. Beginners, who have difficulty in understanding how to do this sequence of movements, can learn it by being guided through the movement. This assistance is gradually reduced until the pupil can perform the movement alone.

Handicapped swimmers, who let themselves fall from a sitting or standing position on the side of the pool into the water, likewise have to master this combined rotation.

6. Diving

The buoyancy, unconsciously experienced as one surfaces during games, is emphasized in this step. Using exercises, such as diving and letting oneself sink to the bottom of the pool, the learner swimmer experiences the surfacing effect and learns how to use it deliberately. The pupil learns how to surface by altering the position of the body and controlling breathing in order to reach the surface and adopt a position where he can breathe easily.

7. Position in the water

At this stage the pupil learns to keep his balance while floating on his back in the pool. Initially, he is supported by the helper, but later learns to keep his balance or to regain it, in spite of turbulence in the water.

8. Gliding

After learning to surface and keep his balance, even in rough water, the pupil is taught how to glide on his own. Initially, he learns to glide passively by being pulled along by his partner. Active gliding comes later on, for example by pushing off from the side of the pool.

9. Movement – Elementary Swimming Movements

As an extension of gliding the pupil now learns to move forward on his own by using his arms and legs. These consist of simple paddling movements.

10. Movement – The First Swimming Style

Moving on from the elementary movements, a swimming stroke technique can be worked out irrespective of the form of handicap. McMillan recommends the normal backstroke using both arms as the simplest form (cf., Hasler-Rietmann, 1976; Weber-Witt, 1993).

1.3.5   The Theory of Integration

Swimming is regarded by many authors (Lorenzen, 1970; Kosel, 1981; Innenmoser, 1988) as an ideal sport for the handicapped, as it allows many of them to move around on their own in the water. While paraplegics and those who cannot walk properly are forced to rely on aids such as wheelchairs and crutches when moving on land, they require no such assistance in the water. Swimming, or moving and playing in the water is also considered as a very suitable sport for the integration of minority groups, to which the handicapped people in our society also belong. Exactly why swimming can be regarded as an integrative sport has not yet been investigated. Perhaps this book might be an incentive for starting a research project on this subject that would look further at it in more depth.

At this point it is worthwhile presenting some basic arguments in favor of swimming as an integrative sport. The theory of "differentiated integration for sport with people with various degrees of handicap" (Rheker, 1996b), as proved and tested over many years of practice, will be outlined fully in the next chapter. We find the following conditions for swimming as a common activity for the handicapped and non-handicapped:

→ **Meeting on a Common Level**
People of various differences come into contact with each other on a common level while swimming and playing in water. When swimming, children and grown-ups, men and women and people with and without handicaps all move around with their heads on the surface of the water, in other words, at the same level. Tall people do not have to look down at smaller people, and those in wheelchairs do not have to look up at pedestrians!

This change in perspective for communication can be felt particularly well if one, just once, has carried out all the daily routine activities in a wheelchair for a whole day. This change in perspective and the distance to other people becomes clear, particularly when speaking to "pedestrians", for example, going shopping or in a busy pedestrian walkway. Since these differing perspectives of looking and talking are absent when moving, playing and swimming in water, there is the chance that one can meet as equals, or perhaps unprejudiced, on the same level and communicate with each other or do things together.

→ **Buoyancy Makes Movements in the Water Easier**
The particular characteristics of water lay the framework down for the fact that people with a handicap do not feel handicapped in the water. The buoyancy that the body experiences in the water permits someone with a serious handicap such as quadriplegia or MS to be able to move much more easily and independently in the water than on land. As almost the whole body (98%-100%) is freed from the force of gravity by

buoyancy, people who can only move very slowly or clumsily on land can now move almost without difficulty. They are no longer limited in their movements compared to the non-handicapped. This applies to people with handicaps such as damage to their joints as well as to those who are overweight or have other handicaps.

→ Learning to Swim in Equal Conditions

Learning to swim lends itself as a particularly suitable activity for gaining integrative experiences. In a group of learners, everyone is in the same situation. No one can swim, but everyone wants to, or should, learn. This means that handicapped and non-handicapped children, in such a group, share the same experiences when playing games in the water. On this basis, further games and exercises, as well as elementary experiences, can be used when learning to swim. This means that both handicapped and non-handicapped children have a similar starting point to enable them to become acquainted with swimming instruction together. When learning other sports such as basketball, gymnastics or soccer, the basis is already very much different, so that these sports, for handicapped and non-handicapped children jointly, cause considerably more problems. Because beginner swimming instruction for non-handicapped children also consists of a lot of games in order to get them used to the water, handicapped children can be included without any problem as well. Interactive and communicative games, as well as games in which no one loses, are particularly suitable for this goal.

→ The Early Beginning of Integration

Integrative sport, as a joint sport for both the handicapped and non-handicapped, should start as early as possible. As prejudices, for example, against minorities manifest themselves in children between four and eight years of age, children of pre-school age should already be given the opportunity of playing jointly with handicapped children. In this way, they get to know handicapped children, without prejudice, as people, so that the handicap as such is not of immediate importance. As beginners swimming shows from results as early as pre-school age, many groups can operate on an integrative basis right from the beginning. In this way, handicapped children will not be excluded at all. Otherwise they would not get to know non-handicapped children. In this way they can learn to treat them in an unprejudiced manner.

→ Integration in Leisure Sport

Swimming as a form of leisure and adventure sport offers ideal opportunities for integration. Any sport that is not so concerned with competition and success can integrate people with various forms of handicap more easily. In competitive sport, those who do not have a lot of ability are often excluded. Opportunities with the motto "games and sport for everybody", on the other hand, make it possible for people with very different physical abilities to join in; old and young, handicapped and non-handicapped, and those with good or not so good physical ability.

All kinds of swimming are suitable for the integration of minority groups, especially the handicapped:

* swimming for beginners is particularly suitable (see previous chapter).
* swimming as a leisure and relaxation activity; holiday time particularly offers opportunities where one is not excluded from leisure activities.
* swimming in public swimming pools, adventure swimming pools, lakes and in the open sea. These open facilities and meeting places offer the opportunity to gain experiences and enjoy organized leisure activities for everybody without exception.
* water gymnastics offer various different goals and perspectives so that heterogeneous groups can take part in activities jointly.
* life-saving swimming, which places particular emphasis on the social objective of "being there for others", also offers the opportunity to integrate handicapped children.
* games with a ball in the water are suitable, especially the variations of the type leading to competitive sport, for letting people of different physical abilities join in.
* diving is a sport, which is gradually, more and more, opening up to handicapped people. (cf., Rheker, U: "Diving with Handicapped People. 1st International Symposium", Paderborn 1997). With a little openness and empathy, many handicapped people can take part in this attractive leisure sport. The fact that, sometimes it can come to an understanding of the reversal of roles "handicapped – non-handicapped" is demonstrated by the example of underwater diving with deaf people. While people with hearing difficulties can converse under water by means of sign language, it is the non-handicapped who do not

understand anything and can only make themselves understood using the few signs of the diver's language.

• health and stamina swimming are especially suitable for people with varying physical abilities.

• swimming as a competitive sport; *competitive* swimming does not need to be organized so that the handicapped and non-handicapped cannot take part. A good example of integration in this area is Britta Siegers, who won several gold medals at the Paralympics and who trains in a top sports swimming club in Cologne with non-handicapped athletes. There are similar examples in water polo for the integration of people with amputated legs.

1.4   Swimming as an Integrative Sport

"When someone dreams alone, it is only a dream.
When many people share the same dream it is the beginning
of a new reality."

(Dom Helder Camara, Brazil)

1.4.1   Introduction

If we look at the various concepts of swimming for beginners, it becomes clear that an overwhelming number of publications have been written for non-handicapped swimmers. Only a few authors (Lorenzen, 1970; Minsel, 1974; Diederley, 1975; Innenmoser, 1988; Lause, 1992) have devoted themselves to the subject of *swimming for the handicapped.* Within this, they place a great deal of importance on the subject of learning to swim for beginners. Similarly, in general publications on sport for the handicapped, the authors, who dominate in publications on swimming for the handicapped, are those following the traditional pedagogical approach for handicapped sport (Gill, 1975; Kodel, 1981; Rieder, 1971) or a medical-therapeutic approach (Van der Schoot, 1976, 1976, 1990; Kosel, 1981, 1988; Innenmoser, 1990 et al.; Rheker, 1996b: 8-12).

The introductory sections of the books cover swimming and learning to swim for specific target groups of the handicapped e.g., swimming for the mentally handicapped (Lause, 1992; Diederley, 1975), swimming for the physically handicapped and people with sensory handicaps (Kosel, 1981; Innenmoser, 1988). Very often the starting point for the concept of swimming by the handicapped is a precise medical diagnosis, and from this adequate techniques suitable for the handicapped are developed using the techniques of swimming for beginners such as diving, breathing, buoyancy, gliding etc. In swimming instruction with handicapped children, a basic knowledge of the types of handicap and their effect on the children's ability to move around is certainly indispensable. This is a point of view that regards children too much from a therapeutic point of view, but which can also conflict with the stimulation of looking at the problem holistically. Many handicapped children are better left to develop their individual ability freely on their own.

Nowadays, there are sports opened up for the handicapped that doctors, to some extent, would advise totally against. For example, diving for handicapped people has reached such a dimension that it has opened up new leisure activities, a new quality of life and much more (cf., Rheker, 1997b).

Swimming and playing in the water particularly offers not only all sorts of rehabilitative and therapeutic opportunities, it also makes it possible to achieve various goals:

- enjoyment at being able to move.
- playing with other people and making social contacts.
- developing new forms of movement and being creative.
- becoming independent and doing things by oneself.
- learning about and increasing one's own abilities.
- getting to know about worthwhile leisure activities.

Swimming, particularly for beginners, is extremely well suited as a practical means of integrating handicapped children and teenagers. In spite of their many differences, which occur even in homogeneous groups of the non-handicapped, people with different physical capabilities have much in common:

- Water as an element, with its various characteristics, (density, pressure, humidity, ability to conduct warmth etc.,) creates new stimuli.
- Water offers the opportunity to learn new motor skills. This is because all children, who want to learn to swim, have either no or very little previous experience. They all want to learn to swim by using the playing method, but none of them has yet mastered the corresponding techniques.
- The basic experiences leading up to actually being able to swim are the same for handicapped and non-handicapped children alike, e.g., experiencing buoyancy and using it in games and exercises etc.
- Swimming offers all sorts of movement experiences, which lead not only to a special swimming technique, but also to many movements and games:
  - being able to dive underwater
  - being able to jump in and dive
  - being able to glide through the water
  - being able to use individual arm and leg techniques etc. (cf., Chapter 2, especially the parts on "Elementary Movements" (2.7) and "Games for Getting Used to the Water" (2.1)).
- The many types of games in swimming for beginners are especially suitable for promoting games with children with various sorts of physical abilities and thus bringing about social contact.

  More arguments in favor of integrative swimming instruction can be found in the various interpretations of swimming (cf., Chapter 1.2).

One decisive argument, however, is the responsibility of the social task of educational institutions such as kindergartens, schools etc. In Germany, for instance, more and more States have taken up the example, which started in Berlin, and are making it possible for children with all kinds of handicap to go to so-called "normal" schools. In the State of North Rhine Westphalia, this was regulated by an edict from its Ministry of Education and Cultural Affairs in 1995. According to this edict, handicapped children are not sent to separate schools for the handicapped. They can choose which school they want to go to, just like any other child.

This, of course, has implications for schools as institutions and also for teacher training and their continuation training. Integrative teaching and integrative sport have to be compulsory subjects in teacher education and their further education. Besides the above arguments for integrative swimming instruction, there are – for schools at least – institutional reasons as well.

Since there are only a few publications or reported experiences on integrative sport and swimming instruction to date, the concept of integrative sport, which has proved itself over twenty years of practice in Paderborn, will be covered in the following sections here. First, we will go into the practice-oriented approach of "differentiated integrative education for sport for people with different physical capabilities" by using the example of the integration of the family in sport. This concept can be used in other areas of sport.

In conclusion, we will cover the basic concept of integrative swimming that has been used in Paderborn. The practice and the organization of this concept will be presented more fully in Chapter 2.

1.4.2 The Various Teaching Theories in Integrated Sport

The Development of the Integrated Concept of Sport
A model was developed from the daily practice of sport with handicapped and non-handicapped people in Paderborn, described as "the theory of teaching various integrated sports to handicapped people" (cf., Rheker, 1996b). Joint sport for handicapped and non-handicapped people has been supervised academically and organizationally by the Department of Sports Science at the University and the Institute of General Tertiary Education, Paderborn since 1977. The following areas of practice have been developed:

* integrated family sport.
* integrated swimming groups.
* integrated wheel-chair sport in various areas:
  * wheelchair sports for children
  * leisure sports
  * table-tennis and badminton
  * basketball in wheelchairs
  * sport for stroke patients
  * swimming with handicapped children and teenagers
  * psychomotor exercises

The different practice areas are carried out primarily in leisure and popular sports, but included also in competitive sport as well. Their use in school sports has also been examined in individual cases. Critical reflection on this practice led to a theory, which builds on the various established experiences in practice. "The connection to the practice and the constant analysis of it gives a further development of the theory, which is oriented to its practical implementation. This is why the portrayal of the practical aspects of various teaching theories for integrated sports acquires a special significance." (Rheker, 1996b).

Basic Anthropological Assumptions

The social situation of the handicapped is still marked by rejection, ostracism, and social reticence (cf., Becker, 1988, Von Bracken, 1981; Jansen, 1981). "We must still reckon on noticeable, negative attitudes. Social integration reaches its true limits based on these." (Speck, 1991). The social integration of the handicapped can be brought a decisive step forward through deliberately planned contact. This is why it is necessary to develop and arrange places for the handicapped and non-handicapped to meet.

Movement, games and sport can provide contact opportunities and thus ways of initiating the integration of the handicapped.

Actual practical sport with the handicapped and the non-handicapped, and the theory it is based on, have the following aims. The attitude of handicapped and non-handicapped people to each other should be changed positively by using the multitude of sporting activities. Social barriers against the handicapped must be highlighted and dismantled, and we should strive for the complete integration of handicapped people in our society.

Integration in sport calls for "the acceptance of each individual human being" (Fediuk, 1992: 19), irrespective of his or her ability, sex, appearance, social status and a possible handicap. This acceptance presupposes a specific personal point of view, which will be described in greater detail in the following basic anthropological statements (cf., Rheker, 1989: 132).

The principles of anthropological acceptance are a basis on which the concept of the different theories of teaching integration in sport is built. Because it has already been described in great detail elsewhere (cf., Rheker, 1996b: 34-39), it will only be mentioned very briefly here:

1. Everybody has a value because he or she is a human being and not because of what he or she can do.
2. Nobody is perfect – weakness and imperfection are part of being human.
3. Everybody has the right to develop his or her individual abilities.
4. Everybody has the right to live in the community and participate in social life.
5. Everybody has the right to decide, in a responsible way, what he or she will do with his or her life.

To summarize, the aim of the different theories of teaching integration in sport for people of various different situations and conditions can be expressed as follows:

"By being able to meet and jointly carrying out activities, games and sport, integration in sports and additional things will be achieved for the handicapped and non-handicapped – people with different circumstances – under positive conditions, so that everybody with his individual abilities and potential will be accepted, and individual development and social integration can be harmonized."

(Rheker, 1996b: 39)

Personal and Social Integration as the Goal of the Various Teaching Theories in Integrated Sports

The practical approach to the various teaching theories in the integration of sport with the handicapped is mainly characterized by the concepts of *individual development* (personal integration) and *social inclusion* (social integration) of each person (cf., Speck, 1991: 301; Rheker, 1995, 1995: 51).

Integration can be portrayed as an ongoing process in which the development of personality and social integration is seen in a reciprocal dependency on each other. The aim of the concept is, on the one hand, personal integration, in the form of the development of the self-image, and with it integration on an individual level (cf., Speck, 1991: 309).

Similarly, social integration is also the aim of the concept, expressed in other terms as integration of the human being in certain social groups, participating in the whole of society, as well as having a social identity (cf., Speck, 1990: 172; Speck, 1991: 309; Rheker, 1995: 51).

If each individual is accepted with his various abilities and circumstances, it is normal to be different (cf., Kanter, 1988: 3; Weizsäcker, 1993: 23). Several authors (Kobi, 1994; Rheker, 1995, 1996b; Speck, 1991) indicate that such an integrative process of this type does not mean the unilateral adjustment of the handicapped to conditions of the society in which they live. Integration must be an interactive process in which both the handicapped and the non-handicapped must change. "Integration should be expressed as a process of mutual adjustment by the integrators and those being integrated." (Kobi, 1994: 76).

"This process should include all aspects of life. Restricting integrative measures, for example, to school (or even just primary school) doesn't mean social integration is achieved. Rather, this approach must be continued throughout all aspects of life: in the family, at school, in the workplace, during leisure and in the community."

(Rheker, 1997a: 396)

The aim of such an integrative sport may therefore be expressed as follows:

"People with different abilities and circumstances (in age, ability, motivation and attitude, whether handicapped or not...) should learn to see and accept others as equal partners, under equal conditions in their activities, play and sports, and to build relationships in society beyond sport."

(Rheker, 1996b: 41)

Dimensions of Integration
When people with different capabilities, e.g., the handicapped and the non-handicapped, come together to participate in common activities, we cannot talk yet about integration in the true sense of the word. Integration is not a condition that is depicted by "an outward, objectivized or relatively impersonal state of affairs" (Kobi, 1994: 75). On the contrary it is a process of mutual reciprocity, which can never be described "as finally completed" (Kobi, 1994: 75). There are various "dimensions" in this process that must be borne in mind.

The following shows the development of a three dimensional model with a horizontal, a vertical and a depth dimension.

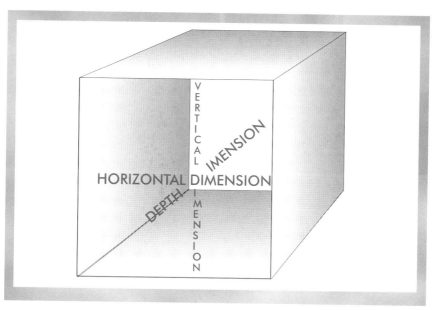

Figure 7: *The Dimensions of Integration*

The Horizontal Dimension of Integration
Various people can come together for an event or for common activities. This applies to people of the same age or to people of different ages, to people of the same or different capabilities, and to the handicapped and the non-handicapped. The outward meeting together of heterogeneous groups or people with different abilities is described as the horizontal dimension of integration.

Various homogeneous or heterogeneous groups can come together in the following way:

- people of the same or different ages.
- people with similar or differing expectations, motives and levels of skill.
- men and women, girls and boys.
- people with the same or different types of handicap.
- people of the same or different background, race and nationality.
- people of the same or different social status.
- handicapped and non-handicapped.

THE HORIZONTAL DIMENSION

- AGE
- SEX
- EXPECTATIONS
- MOTIVES AND LEVELS OF ABILITY
- STATUS
- NATIONALITY
- THEIR ROLE MODELS OR IDEALS
- FORMS OF HANDICAP
- THE HANDICAPPED AND THE NON-HANDICAPPED

Figure 8: *Horizontal Dimensions*

The meetings can take place on a single occasion such as an integrative games festival or on a regular basis such as homogeneous sports groups of handicapped, or in integrated sports groups. The heterogeneity of these groups initially enables only one conclusion about the organizational participation of people with various physical abilities (the horizontal dimension of integration), but not about the intensity of relationships, the emotional quality of experiences, and equally not about the depth of relationships between the various generations or forms of handicap etc.

If integration as a process, which also leads to changes in attitude, is to be initiated, this needs to be more than just superficial meetings. Contact with the handicapped does not automatically lead to positive attitudes. This requires more favorable circumstances (cf., Cloerkes, 1985: 224, 489).

The Vertical Dimension of Integration

The vertical dimension of integration means the quality of social relationships between people of varying and different circumstances, which lead to processes so that everyone in a heterogeneous group – and especially the handicapped – is accepted and integrated. "Social integration is the result of appropriate interaction between handicapped and non-handicapped people." (Schuchardt, 1994: 207).

If integration is to take place beyond the horizontal dimension, and if intense social relationships in the vertical dimension are to be achieved, a number of positive conditions must be fulfilled:

THE VERTICAL DIMENSION

- OPENNESS
- VOLUNTARY CONTACT
- A POSITIVE BASIC ATTITUDE
- TOLERANCE
- COMMON GOALS AND TASKS
- PERSONAL INVOLVEMENT
- IDEALS/MODELS
- AN ENVIRONMENT OF EMOTIONAL EXPERIENCES
- THE INTENSITY OF RELATIONSHIPS

Figure 9: *The Vertical Dimension*

A complete description of the vertical dimension of integration has already been made elsewhere (cf., Rheker, 1996b: 46-50, 63-72).

The Depth Dimension of Integration
The vertical dimension described in the previous chapter can be carried out in various groups – in homogenous as well as in heterogeneous groups. Because, by personal involvement and working towards common goals and on common tasks with openness and tolerance etc., relationships in groups of the same age or with the same abilities, e.g., in a youth soccer team, or in "sporting groups with the same type of handicap", become so intensive that the vertical dimension for these people is achieved.

The bringing together of heterogeneous groups is a deciding feature for the concept of integrated teaching developed here. If people of various ages, sex, types of handicap, handicapped and non-handicapped come together for the purpose of carrying out common activities, the quality of integration is deepened and intensified by the interaction of different target groups, which can be shown in a third dimension – the depth dimension (cf., Figure 10).

People of various ages, with different expectations, motives and levels of skill, from various social-economic groups (status), nationals and foreigners, men and women, boys and girls, people with various different types of handicap and the handicapped and non-handicapped do not just meet at integrative sports events on a single occasion and only superficially at the horizontal level.

They see themselves and the others through the criteria of the vertical dimension (openness, the voluntary nature of the contact, positive attitude, tolerance, common goals and tasks, personal involvement, models/ideals, the quality of the experience and the intensity of the experience) so intensely that close relationships develop beyond these various levels (generation, status etc). This is so, especially between people with various different types of handicap and the non-handicapped (cf., Rheker, 1996b: 46-52).

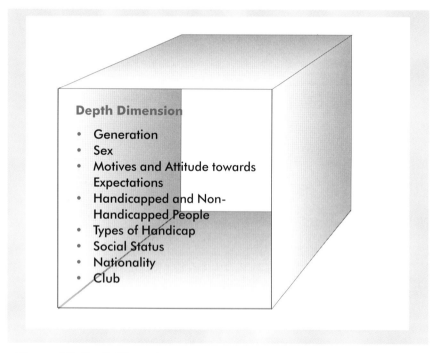

Depth Dimension

- Generation
- Sex
- Motives and Attitude towards Expectations
- Handicapped and Non-Handicapped People
- Types of Handicap
- Social Status
- Nationality
- Club

Figure 10: *Depth Dimension*

1.4.3   Integration in Family Sports

Origin and Conception
The integrative family sports group was founded in Paderborn on 12th June 1982. The group has now increased in size to more than 50 families. It meets every second and fourth Saturday in the month at the University sports hall.

Many different kinds of people come to play, sing and dance and play together – toddlers, children, young people, adults and elderly people, the handicapped and non-handicapped, locals, foreigners, etc. Sometimes more than 100 people take part in family sport.

In addition to family sport, there are many common activities such as family leisure activities, walks, sports festivals etc. In 1990, the TuRa Elsen Family Sports Group was awarded the German "Sports Prize for the Handicapped" for its model of an exemplary integrative sports group (cf., Rheker, 1995: 57f).

The integrative sports group in Paderborn, Germany was developed from the joint sporting activities of families with handicapped children and families with non-handicapped, and was founded to carry out this type of practice. As a result, families with children of varying degrees of handicap meet to play sport together with families with non-handicapped children since the day of its foundation. The "Paderborn Model", for integrative sport, does not seek to be, nor is it supposed to be a "model, one-off exception". Rather it seeks to function beyond the integration experienced in the family sports group e.g., in the working together of the TuRa Elsen Club with clubs and organizations in the immediate area (the Town Sports Club, the District Gymnastic Club, local authorities etc.) (cf., Rheker, 1995: 138).

In close cooperation with the Department of Sports Science at the University of Paderborn, the general facilities provided for the Integrative Family Sports Group are very good. There is a triple sports hall complex and a gymnastics room available, so that after the start of each sports session, the participants can be divided up into four smaller groups. The availability of equipment (parachutes, roller boards, trampolines etc.) in the meanwhile, can be called almost ideal.

Activities in the Family Sports Group

The methods of teaching the various ways of integration in sport for people with varying abilities have been developed from the everyday practice of integrative family sport. This is why it is possible to show how this concept works in practice. Several phases of each session, i.e., the beginning and end of each of the sports session, are dedicated to joint activities by all the participants of this large, heterogeneous group (cf., social integration).

In the middle section there are different activities for the various target groups (cf., personal integration). Besides this "normal lesson structure", there are a few, specially programmed sports afternoons i.e., "project sessions", and other activities such as swimming, walking, sports festivals, family leisure periods inter alia (cf., Rheker, 1966b: 55-61).

Figure 11: *The phases of the activities in integrated family sport*

Joint Sports Sessions: Games and Sports for Everybody
Attempts are being made to implement the motto of the German Sports Federation "Sports for Everybody" in two ways; many different target groups such as children, teenagers and adults, nationals and foreigners, handicapped and non-handicapped people, should all have the opportunity to join together in family sport. They should not, however, be divided into separate groups or clubs to play sports. Rather, they should be offered the opportunity to meet other people while taking part in activities, sport and games and to perform these activities jointly together. Each family sports session should begin and end with everybody playing, singing, dancing, performing gymnastics and other movement-based games (cf., Rheker, 2000 (English version): 84-132; Integration through Games and Sports: Part B1: "Movement, Games and Sports for the Whole Family").

Various Sports Activities

In order that everybody, with their different circumstances in such a large heterogeneous group, can fulfill their personal needs and expectations in the field of sport, in at least a part of the sports session, the group is divided into four different groups after the initial joint phase. This gives each person the opportunity to develop on an individual basis. The participants are divided up according to age and target group. Physical ability or handicap is not a deciding factor.

(1) Various Activities for Parents

In one section of the hall the parents have an opportunity to put into practice their own ideas about movement, sport and games. Here they can develop their abilities without having to worry about their children, whether they are handicapped or not. In many conversations it has become clear that, besides the motive of wanting to do something for one's health and physical condition, or to get a break from stress, the social motive is the focal point for the parents, especially mothers. It is very important for them to sit down and talk to other like-minded people and exchange ideas.

The exercise instructor lets the parents decide on the content of the sessions. In this way they get to do relaxation training, gymnastics, stretching, back exercises (gymnastics for the spine), and play games like badminton or volleyball, changing over from one to the other freely.

(2) Various Activities for Handicapped and Younger, Non-Handicapped Children

In another part of the hall there are special activities for handicapped and the younger, non-handicapped children in order to encourage them and let them pursue their own particular goals. *Integration* is placed very much in the foreground as a goal for younger children when handicapped and non-handicapped children move around and play games together. Another goal is the *development of individual abilities* and *skills* (cf. personal integration) by doing specific activities from the motor pedagogic and psychomotor areas for *physical, material and social experience.*

Independence is another goal for the younger children, especially the handicapped ones. For many children, this can be clearly interpreted as a process of gaining independence from their parents. Through regular family sports activities, the *interest in sports* is also developed or increased.

For this target group, three points of emphasis can be set for practice:

1. Trampoline gymnastics (see Rheker, 1995: 139-151).
2. Sport and obstacle gymnastics (see Rheker, 1995: 149-151).
3. Games for physical, material and social experience (see Rheker, 1995: 113-132).

(3) Various Activities for Young Handicapped People and Older Non-Handicapped Children

With this target group, the aim, in the varied part of the sports session, is to let the children fulfill their expectations when playing the games and sports on offer. It can be left up to them whether they either romp around or concentrate seriously on a sporting activity.

The older children and teenagers often have to watch out for their younger or handicapped brothers and sisters as a daily routine. For this reason they enjoy the freedom to develop their own sport. When exercising, they can, therefore, fulfill their individual wishes and do things they like, such as playing in pedal-cars, skateboarding, playing table tennis, doing the high jump or trampolining. However, they often prefer to play some games more seriously rather than just romp around, e.g., indoor hockey, soccer or badminton. When they play these sports, the small fathers' group often joins in.

(4) Differentiated Activities for the Crawling Tiny Tots

As the number of families, with toddlers aged from one to five in the family group has grown, another form of activity has been developed for the middle phase of the session. These groups frequently meet in the gymnastics room but also sometimes play in one of the three gymnasium halls, when, for example, the gymnastics room is occupied by other parents doing relaxation exercises. The tiny tots in this group like best to play the following games: singing or playing in a circle, games with psycho-motor aids or gymnastic equipment and games that promote physical, material or social experiences.

Project Sessions

Not every family sports session goes according to the plan laid down, with joint activities at the beginning and end of each session and a variety of activities in the middle. Some sports afternoons are arranged as project sessions that are given a particular motto. Proven themes for such sessions are the circus, jungle adventures, the sports studio, Desert Island or a project in keeping with the time of year, such as Christmas or carnival.

With a little bit of effort, the sports hall can be set up appropriately beforehand, e.g., a parachute can be used to make a circus tent in which the circus events take place. A sports studio can be set up with a video camera etc., or the gymnasium hall can be decorated as a setting for Christmas or winter games.

The project session begins with an introduction to the theme with everybody present. Then various workshops are held, in which young and old can take part, e.g., the circus program can be worked out and rehearsed, such as groups working on parts for clowns, wild animal trainers, acrobats, tight-rope walkers etc. The workshops are led by the exercise instructors or parents with previous experience so that everybody can contribute to the success of the program. At the end, all the contributions are put together to form a colorful program. A complete circus or a sports studio is now presented "live" (cf., Rheker, 1993: 134-138).

More Activities for the Family Sports Group

Many joint activities done as a sport or within the sports session can ensure that the integrative family sports group, with its various members, grows closer together. Contacts between the group members are thus deepened and, above all, new members get the opportunity to bond into the group more quickly and intensively. These activities include:

* family leisure activities.
* sports festivals.
* walks.
* swimming.
* joint activities together with TuRa Elsen.

1.4.4 Integrative Sports for Wheelchair-bound Children

In the children's wheelchair group – the Paderborn Ahorn-Panther e.V., children with various handicaps (spina bifida, those unable to walk properly, the mentally handicapped etc.) carry out movement, games and sport together with non-handicapped children. In order that this takes place under equal conditions, the non-handicapped children who normally don't use wheelchairs also use these when playing. Sports wheelchairs are such an attractive plaything and piece of sports equipment for non-handicapped children that there are sometimes not enough to go around to satisfy demand, although just under twenty have recently been acquired.

The following main things are emphasized during wheelchair sports for children:

- games to train children how to use a wheelchair.
- integrative games.
- gymnastics.
- preparation for various sports such as table tennis, badminton, wheelchair basketball and wheelchair dancing.
- trying new sports such as "quad rugby", wheelchair orienteering races etc.

Following on to play wheelchair basketball and wheelchair table tennis with the grown-ups is very easy for the teenagers, because both these groups play directly after the children's group in the Ahorn Sports Park, and so the teenagers can play in both groups.

Each session begins with games that are fun to play and that interest everybody. Besides games demanding skill in a wheelchair (tag, obstacle course etc.), emphasis is placed on games designed to encourage children with varying physical abilities to play together, e.g., games with a parachute, movement games with music or ball games. Afterwards, there are playful games to practice proper gymnastics exercises in a wheelchair.

In later stages of the sports section, the children can also introduce and try out their ideas and needs for movement, games and sports, e.g., little games based on major sports: basketball, handball, badminton, table tennis, squash inter alia.

By means of joint movement, games and sports activities, the participants develop an understanding for the situation of the others. The children learn quickly to accept others the way they are, even with their unique similarities and differences.

This breaks down the social distance between the handicapped and the non-handicapped and creates an atmosphere in which everybody encounters others as human beings: the handicapped are not seen as "the deficient". These encounters between handicapped and non-handicapped children have lead to firm friendships.

However, the above process of integration is not restricted to children. The children's group of the Ahorn-Panthers meets to play sport in the "Ahorn Sports Park". This is a large sports center with four gymnastics halls, athletics fields and ten squash courts laid out next to each other so that everyone can – visually at least – take part in the sports activities of the other groups. In this way we experience a natural 'togetherness' and 'joint feeling' between our so-called "handicapped sports groups" and the other sports groups.

The integrative children's wheelchair groups often receive visits from various groups such as school classes, scout groups, company groups etc., which come not only to observe our interesting sports groups, but also to take active part in the games. Many of these children remain in contact with these groups. Subsequently, for example, it was possible to plan a camp with the scouts and hold it at Whitsun.

Parental Work and Other Activities
While the children and teenagers are playing sport with their instructors, the parents meet in the Ahorn Sports Park restaurant, which is separated from the sports facility by only a glass door. There they can exchange experiences, talk about common problems, plan things together and give each other tips on how to deal with the authorities and school governing bodies. The parents have thus been able to help others prevent their children being sent away to special schools for the handicapped. They have also, despite resistance, got their children accepted at normal schools.

Additional Activities
Some additional activities ensure that the social environment is integrated into the sports group, thereby broadening the children's range of social experience:

- family leisure periods: once a year the children's wheelchair group organizes a joint event with family and friends e.g., at the handicapped association's clubrooms at the Emmer Lake in Schieder-Schwalenberg.
- trying out leisure activities such as mini-golf, rowing, boating, walking or hiking.
- besides the summer festival there are other occasions to get together to have a party or a barbecue.

Such activities offer many opportunities (from the preparation to actually carrying them out and analyzing the results) for the handicapped and the non-handicapped to meet. There are opportunities to get to know what it is like to be handicapped, and this can lead to a change of attitude on the part of one group about the other (Rheker, 1996b: 86-88, 1997a).

1.4.5   The Concept of Integrated Swimming

Origin

In Paderborn since 1977, it has been possible for handicapped and non-handicapped children and teenagers to be able to learn to swim. This project was initiated by active sports students as well as by the sports teacher Dr Uwe Rheker. Teenagers with various forms of handicap were to have the opportunity to learn to enjoy movement in the water by using games and other basic motor experiences, and thus become able to move around independently in the water and to learn to swim.

Right from the beginning, social integration was the aim of the lesson. Through the participation of non-handicapped brothers, sisters, friends and parents, this aim was turned into reality. Today, some 30-40 handicapped children and teenagers come with their companions and helpers to a weekly swimming session, so that at times up to 100 people are present at the "swimming with handicapped children and teenagers" lessons. This large group was therefore divided up so that it is possible to learn to swim at either one of two separate times.

The group was under the care of students of the Sports Science Department from the University of Paderborn right from the beginning. This allowed each of the seriously handicapped children to be given individual attention. Initially all the children belonged to the Paderborn Handicapped Sports

Group. Through the increase in the number of sporting activities also available from the Paderborn Ahorn-Panthers and the TuRa Elsen clubs, handicapped adolescents are now accepted by all of these three clubs. The three clubs cover the medical insurance and their sports activities are subsidized as a therapy by the national health insurance scheme.

The Concept
From the swimming lessons with handicapped children and teenagers a concept for "the various teaching theories in sport for people with varying degrees of physical ability" was developed in a similar fashion to the way integrative family sport was started.

Although the children in the swimming group were initially organized by a club devoted only to doing sport for the disabled and the physically handicapped, all the children, irrespective of handicap, were accepted from the start. For this reason, right up to now, many people with many different forms of handicap are together in the group; the mentally handicapped and many of the physically handicapped forms (spastics, spina bifida, paraplegics, muscular dystrophy, dysmelia etc.) as well as multiple handicapped adolescents. This variety is completed by pupils from the schools for children with learning difficulties and those with behavioral problems.

In order to implement the aim of integration, non-handicapped brothers, sisters and friends, as well as the parents and helpers of the handicapped children were deliberately involved from the beginning. In the meanwhile, the older helpers, who have since become sports teachers, and who have kept in contact with the swimming group, bring their own children along as well. The main aim of the integrative swimming concept can also be viewed the same way as it is for other branches of integrated sport:

"For people with varying physical abilities, being able to meet freely and by using joint activities in movement, games and sport, also including swimming, integration in sport and in other areas of society will be achieved. This must be done in such a manner that each person, with his or her own different abilities, will have the opportunity to develop as an individual and thus be integrated socially."

(cf., Rheker, 1996b: 39)

Social integration and individual development (personal integration) should be related to each other and be mutually dependent (cf., Rheker, 1996b: 41). This goal is being achieved in the Paderborn swimming concept in the following way; every session begins with games designed to promote *social integration*. Later on in the session the handicapped children and teenagers have the opportunity to develop their ability to swim and play in the water. During this part they normally receive individual attention.

Games for Everybody
The joint games at the beginning of the session take place in the learner's pool so that everybody without exception can join in. These are simple, popular games or variations of well-known games, of which the following are especially suitable:

- *running* and *catching* games such as "Fisherman, fisherman how deep is the water?", "Who's afraid of the big White Shark?", "Chain-Catch" or "Magic Mouse" etc
- circle and singing games such as "Eeny Miny Mo" or "Show us your feet"
- *small ball games* such as Hunter's ball, Party ball, Duck hunting or Tiger ball etc

These games can be played by everybody:

- handicapped and non-handicapped children and teenagers
- people with various forms of handicap
- swimmers and non-swimmers
- children and adults
- locals and foreigners

By playing together, the participants get to know and learn to accept the abilities and skills of the others. The games help them to develop a better relationship with each other. This breaks down their social detachment to the handicapped and they experience them as individuals with their own characteristics and abilities. The swimming session can also finish with joint games.

Photo 1: *Each swimming session begins with joint games.*

Individual Stimulation

The individual development of the personality of each and every handicapped and non-handicapped is catered for in this concept by **individual attention**. Each handicapped child gets – at least at the beginning – a personal carer, who looks after the child with its individual abilities, and who is able to take care of the child's individual problems. This individual care is especially necessary for seriously handicapped and very nervous children. By getting used to the carer a bond of trust grows, and this enables also children with problems to achieve the aims of elementary swimming, such as diving, breathing, floating etc.

This creates the basis for learning techniques that allow them to move around independently in the water.

After an intensive period of getting used to the water in the areas of:

- playful games to get used to the water
- underwater diving
- breathing

- jumping in and diving
- floating
- gliding
- elementary swimming movements

The children can then be brought on to learn individual swimming techniques.

Emphasis is placed on the rapid learning of a swimming technique. Above all, the children should experience the fun and pleasure of moving in the water, and by playing together make social contact with others by and discover swimming as a possible leisure activity.

For many children, swimming is the only sport in which they can move without any assistance, thus exercising their circulatory system and doing something for their own health. For this reason **teaching** the children **to become independent** is a further, important aim, which can be pursued by learning to swim. It begins with getting changed, where only as much assistance as necessary should be given. Anything that makes the children independent should be applied, and they should be made to do these things by themselves, even if it takes a little longer. This applies also in the same way to smaller non-handicapped children. Taking a shower and going to the toilet before and after swimming are both parts of the swimming instruction and should be included in the program. "Getting into the water" can also be developed into a learning process in the program towards independence. For example paraplegic children or those with cerebral palsy can be carried into the water initially. However, later on during their swimming experiences, they can be taken out of their wheelchairs and sat on the edge of the pool. From there they can get into the water by themselves, at first with assistance, which is then later reduced in steps very gradually. When they can swim by themselves, they let themselves drop in forwards (lateral rotation) and immediately turn into a safe position onto their backs (vertical rotation).

Individual Swimming Techniques
In the development of swimming techniques for some forms of handicap, one cannot start with the usual techniques of competitive swimming such as crawl, backstroke, breaststroke or butterfly stroke.

So even while the child is getting used to the water, the instructor needs to find out which movements the child can already perform, and which movements will give the child the ability to move forward and permit surfacing.

Deficient movements, such as the crawl leg stroke of, for example a spastically handicapped child, can be amplified by using flippers, giving forward movement and letting the child able to move in the water by itself. In order to breathe freely, it is easier for many handicapped children and teenagers to develop their own swimming techniques while gliding on their backs.

Photo 2: *K-D has been swimming by himself for many years now.*

Swimming techniques can also be learnt by jumping in or diving into a prone position.

Photo 3: *Some children like swimming in a prone position.*

Helpers

The helpers in the Paderborn swimming group with handicapped children and teenagers are mostly students of Sports Science. During their sports teacher training courses for various school levels, (Primary, Secondary I and Secondary II), or as graduate students of Sports Science, they can gain practical experience in the theory and practice of sport with the handicapped. They are able to attend seminars in Sport for the Handicapped and Integrative Sport and, at the same time, complete a course of practical teaching in the various areas of sports for the handicapped:

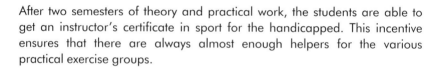

- integrated family sport
- integrated children's wheelchair sport
- integrated leisure sports for wheelchairs and pedestrians
- swimming with handicapped children and teenagers

After two semesters of theory and practical work, the students are able to get an instructor's certificate in sport for the handicapped. This incentive ensures that there are always almost enough helpers for the various practical exercise groups.

Many helpers stay with their sports groups longer than just the two compulsory semesters, as often an intensive and personal relationship develops between them and the swimmer pupils they work with, which sometimes goes far beyond sport.

Another reliable source of potential helpers are those doing community service (as an alternative to military service). The Paderborn Sports Association for sport has employed two such people for handicapped children and teenagers. They are not only employed as helpers in looking after the various sports groups of handicapped teenagers, they are able also to take over driving duties in some cases. Two people, doing their community service from the Institute of Sports Medicine, fill up the numbers to provide helpers for the swimming sessions.

Senior school pupils, active Scout or youth group members are also able, after suitable training, to be used as helpers for handicapped children or teenagers. If there are still not enough helpers, parents can also be used to assist. Of course, it is advisable for parents not to look after their own children, as learning difficulties can often occur this way. Over-cautious parents inhibit the child's learning process, as can happen with parents who expect too much of their children, or exert too much pressure on them to succeed, thus preventing them from achieving the desired learning success.

Photo 4: *Practicing the leg kick is easier when done together.*

Working in Small Groups

As soon as the children and teenagers have got rid of most of their fears, or are capable of moving around in the water, more or less independently, children with the same abilities can be put together in a small group. These "mini-groups" require only one helper. Even so, we also put children with varying abilities together so that they can play together after the games at the beginning and before the end of the session. Thus little games in the water are done in a part of the pool, where the children, with varying disabilities and abilities and non-handicapped children can play together (see Photo 4).

The opportunity is taken to change over the helpers when doing competitions in order to effect new aims in swimming and games. Relay games are particularly suitable:

- swimming relays
- diving relays
- clothes changing relays (T-shirts)
- relay races carrying objects

1.5 Fear

"Do not be afraid of walking forwards slowly, be afraid of standing still."

(Taiwanese Proverb)

The Role of Fear in Learning to Swim

Learning to swim and, in particular, learning to dive is associated with fear for many beginners. Although not mentioned or played down in many books about swimming for beginners, fear, while learning various movements in the unfamiliar element of water, is a decisive factor.

At the same time, the role fear plays in situations containing moments of danger may be regarded as quite positive. It keeps an inexperienced climber in the mountains from putting himself and others unnecessarily into danger. Equally, it teaches those learning to swim not to enter cold, deep water recklessly when they can no longer stand up in it. But, if the fear grows, it can influence the learning of new movements considerably by blocking them out or cramping up the mind.

Therefore, one of the aims of the instruction for beginners swimming is to make them aware of any fears existing, so that they can learn and inwardly digest them, thus ensuring that they do not let them inhibit the learning process. "Scientific studies confirm that the conquering of fear and progress in learning to swim run parallel" (Wilke, 1979: 28). But fear can also inhibit the learning of various movements, or even cause learning blockages to the extent that the pupil literally "jumps out of the water".

Behavioral Characteristics of Fear

In order to make it easier to recognize the signs of fear, a few examples of the types of fear are described here:

* inhibited movements
* a stiff, cramped posture
* tensed muscles to the point of cramp
* children not letting go of the helper's hand, but holding on to it in a cramp-like and tight manner
* physiological reactions: accelerated breathing and an increased heartbeat

- a fixed facial expression
- unnatural and artificial laughter (in contrast to open and happy laughter, an inhibited, embarrassed smile is sometimes noticeable in nervous children)
- verbal comments: "I'm scared", "I've got wobbly knees", "I feel sick", "I've got to go to the toilet"
- a constant need to empty the bladder
- nausea to the point of vomiting in the water (cf., Wilke, 1979: 28)

These symptoms should be taken seriously, no pressure should be exerted and games should be used to divert the anxious child's attention away from his fears. As there is often a deep-rooted reason for a swimmer's fear, an attempt should be made to recognize those situations that give rise to it. If this is successful, it is possible to work on the causes of fear and gradually break it down. However, very often the children cannot talk about the causes of their fear. Very small children or children with various forms of handicap (the mentally handicapped inter alia) are not able to describe or analyze the situations that give rise to their anxieties.

In this context, it is important that the swimmer pupil is not confronted with more than he can cope with, and that he feels 100% safe and gradually learns where he can have confidence in himself. GABLER describes a positive aim of swimming for beginners as being "the overcoming of the fear of water through positive experiences and understanding, so that they actually like going into the water, and they don't come to avoid it" (1977: 124). Assistance in overcoming the learner's fear can be given by getting them to play games in shallow water, such as games played in a circle or singing in the water, running or catching games, little ball games, and games with toys etc.

Anxious Behavior and Overcoming Fear

Wilke keeps the phenomenon of fear separate from anxiety, which he subscribes to visible causes. "In cases of such recognizable, concrete causes, psychologists talk about anxiety rather than fear" (1979: 28). As fear is described in everyday language as the fear of real threats, e.g., fear of heights, fear of the dark, fear of storms etc., we shall make a clear distinction in the rest of this book. Wilke divides this fear into five categories according to its causes:

- fear of visible failure, of making oneself look silly in front of others
- fear of the teacher
- fear of the depth or breadth of water
- fear of swallowing water
- fear of the threat of water (Wilke, 1979: 28)

Fear of Failure

Adult non-swimmers often try to conceal their lack of ability to swim from friends and relatives, and therefore avoid situations in which their lack of ability might become apparent. Instead of a holiday at the beach, they prefer to go "into the mountains" and tend to avoid other opportunities such as a visit to the swimming pool or partaking in water sports.

For non-swimmers, the aim is to remove the fear of looking foolish in public and give them the opportunity to admit that they cannot swim, in a stress-free atmosphere. If they can be offered, for example, a course for "like-placed adult non-swimmers", it would perhaps be possible to overcome their fears and mental blocks by having a little learning success. Sometimes these people get the opportunity to take the first steps to learn to swim together with their children in a parent-and-child swimming course.

Fear of the Instructor

"Strict instructors", instructors with an energetic teaching manner or instructors with high expectations of their pupil's performance can – especially in children – cause learning blocks, anxiety and timorous, cramped behavior in the water.

For beginners swimming, instructors who show understanding for putting over primarily the fun and joy of moving in the water, are those who subsequently achieve positive teaching success in swimming techniques. For this reason, the aims of swimming for beginners should consist mainly of bringing out the fun aspects of playing and movement in the water, introducing various types of movement with and without aids, with and without music etc., and thus overcoming existing anxieties and working out a repertoire of movements for learning swimming techniques.

Fear of Deep Water

The fear of deep water is shown in the great insecurity felt when the swimmer's feet leave firm ground. But it also begins when breathing is made more difficult by the pressure of water in chest-deep water, which can cause a feeling of being closed in and of fear. Equally, water buoyancy in shallow water can influence stability even when standing upright, so that minor turbulence can lead to insecurity and a loss of balance and hence to feelings of fear.

Fear of deep water can be so intense that pupils consciously or unconsciously forget their swimming kit in order not to have to take part in the lesson.

One female school pupil, at a school for mentally handicapped children, was so afraid of deep water that she was given to vomiting. With a lot of encouragement, a build up of her self-confidence and "gentle persuasion", this fear was overcome initially in visibly shallow water. The deciding factor here was the close attention paid by her teacher and her helper, so that the girl was able to hold on to the side of the pool with both hands initially in shallow water. Later on, one hand was taken away. With the help of a partner she could finally be led by both hands into open water. The assistance of the partner was gradually reduced in small steps, and after a while the girl could wade through the water by herself.

A little later on still, she was able to take her legs off the bottom of the pool by being pulled on her back and thus gradually into the swimming position, which prepared her for deeper water.

However, after the summer vacation there was an obvious retrograde situation with clearly recognizable symptoms of fear, which again had to be overcome in small steps.

Fear of deep water often manifests itself again when children have already been taught elementary swimming movements (crawl or breaststroke) and then have to carry these out in deep water. In such cases there are proven methods by which the anxious pupil can be got used to deep water. This should not be done, at all costs, by tricking the pupil into swimming in deep water. Methods and aids to help are:

- swimming along the side of the pool
- swimming with somebody else
- swimming from one corner of the pool to the other. By this we mean from the side of the pool in the corner to the adjacent side. The distance, which can be freely chosen at the start, is gradually increased.

Fear of the Width of the Pool

This fear manifests itself with many learners already at a very early phase of beginning to swim. Most beginners don't have enough confidence to glide away from the side of the pool into the open water in the middle. It is therefore advisable to get the pupil to begin slowly and lead up in small steps to gliding freely.

Initial exercises in passive gliding should be carried out with body-contact. At first, a partner pulls the other, keeping quite close to the pupil's body and giving a lot of support. By slowly separating away from the partner, e.g., gliding in the wake caused by the separation, the way is opened for the pupil to be able to glide on his own. This is done towards a solid object such as the edge of the pool or the steps. The first stage away from the edge of the pool into "the open pool" can be made easier by having the pupil glide towards somebody standing close by.

As the distance covered by the pupil on his own increases, the helper's assistance can gradually be reduced until it is only necessary for safety and orientation purposes.

Another cause for fear when gliding alone in water lies in the insecurity felt by inexperienced children – and sometimes also adult swimmers – because they have not learned how to resume a standing position after coming out of the gliding position. For this reason, coming into a standing position from a gliding position must be deliberately practiced. With the help of a partner, the pupil first tries to bend his legs under his body from the gliding position and assume a standing position. Later he uses his arms to support this movement by pressing them downwards and to the rear.

If the pupils have already mastered a swimming technique, the fear of the width of the seemingly large pool can be reduced. This can be done to start with by getting them to do short distances towards clearly visible goals, such as a line, the edge of the pool or a partner etc., and then gradually increase the distance to be covered in tiny steps.

Fear of Swallowing Water

Almost every swimmer has been embarrassed at least once, by wanting to inhale when not above the surface of the water. As a result, a wave of water enters the mouth, and he ends up 'swallowing' water. Water forcing its way into the breathing passages can cause a strong coughing attack. Such experiences can be very unpleasant, particularly for the beginner swimmer, and can cause acute breathing problems. Children and adults, who have learned the right breathing techniques, are well prepared for the danger of swallowing water. Exercises, including the technique of exhaling water against the pressure while underwater, can be found in Chapter 2, in the section on Breathing (Chapter 2.3).

The General Fear of the Threat from Water

The general fear of the threat from water can have many causes. Often it is over-cautious parents, perhaps having themselves not overcome their own fear of water, who, with their well intended tips, are responsible for the children's anxious attitude. If the possible dangers are portrayed in a dramatic fashion, these fears can be even reinforced. In swimming instruction for very small children, the practice of not letting anxious parents take part in the lessons has proved itself, because the children learn more quickly to move in water without any fear. Similarly, over- demands and expectations of the child's performance on the part of the parents can cause fear of swimming in their children.

Lack of familiarization with water is the "most frequent reason for the general fear of water during the first swimming lessons" (Wilke, 1979: 33). It is therefore particularly important to make this familiarization interesting, by using a lot of games and exercises, which emphasize the fun aspect of games and movement in the water as well as playing with others (cf., Chapter 2.1). If the process of familiarization with water can take place in ideal environmental conditions (in a manageable area, with lots of play equipment etc), and if success is achieved following encouragement from the side (praise, recognition) and reaches even self-praise (cf., also Chapter 1.7), even anxious beginners can overcome their fears and learn to move around in water by themselves. In this way, anxious swimmers become courageous swimmers, who feel at ease in water and can swim, dive and play safely.

1.6   Motivation (H. Böhmer)

"Kind words achieve more than angry cursing."

(German Proverb)

For young people, learning to swim is, for the most part, a start into a completely new environment. This new 'world' is also filled with fresh experiences in movement and new demands in learning.

A New Environment

Experience shows that learning about water, as a new environment to move around in, has a high degree of attraction for children – children actually want to go into the water! Their inquisitive behavior serves to familiarize them with the unknown and to transform risk into security (Cube, 1990). This is based on the theory that only an ideal degree of exploration can be achieved when an ideal degree of security is present. A prerequisite of this theory is that a high degree of "mobile" security is needed to permit such inquisitiveness in an unfamiliar environment. That is to say, when the swimming pool cannot be 'taken home', the child should bring along as many "old acquaintances" as possible for his first encounter with the new environment. Children should certainly be accompanied by someone they trust and bring some of their toys, preferably those capable of being used in water. These elements of a familiar environment help create a high degree of readiness to explore. The space in which they are to move should also be reconnoitered in small, easily understood steps in order to avoid any large degree of insecurity.

The beginners must not experience the new environment as cold or unfriendly. First of all, how will they find the temperature? The newcomer to the water must encounter temperatures, in as well as out of the water, that he finds comfortable, thus allowing him the opportunity to investigate everything fully. These positive conditions can also be created for older beginners. For example, familiar music can ease an adult's first steps into the water.

Fresh Experiences in Movement

The very first experiences in water, based on playful familiarization, open up a huge repertoire of fresh movement experiences to the beginner. The perception that one's own body is responsible for creating these movement experiences goes along with the satisfaction of the urge for "self-inducement" (Deci & Ryan, 1985). A feeling of "flow" (Csikscentmihalyi, 1996) is quite possible at this phase. The flow experience relates to the pleasurable state of engaging in an activity quite unaware of time or oneself.

The feeling of self-inducement and the "flow" phenomenon can be both a part of, and a condition of the *intrinsically motivated* learning processes. We speak of intrinsically motivated behavior when it happens on its own, i.e., when a person acts on his own impetus (Rheinberg, 1995: 137). We differentiate this motivation from so-called extrinsically motivated behavior, where the motivation to do something comes more from outside, that is to say as the result of an act, which is to be seen more as a result of that action.

How can this knowledge be applied to swimming? The first experiences of movement in water must take place in a playful fashion. If the swimmer feels comfortable in "playful activity", and he does not feel overtaxed and feels that he is playing in the water, rather than being a plaything of the water, this lays the basis for intrinsically motivated behavior. This motivation effect is especially appreciated, when involvement with an object for as long as possible is intended. So, if the aim of instruction for beginners is to experience water as a life-long pleasure, the instructor should try to create the basic conditions for intrinsically motivated behavior in the water.

New Learning Demands

Learning to swim means learning in the water, and learning to live in a new element. To a large extent there are also kinesthetic aspects as well as cognitive aspects of learning. The beginner feels what sort of effect pressure or drag, exerted by individual parts of the body, has on the water. The beginner learns for the first time to perceive the buoyancy of his own body – to use it or to overcome it. Because of these complex elementary learning demands, it seems advisable to avoid too heavy an aim in the initial stages of learning to swim, so that children can fulfil their own expectations.

Self-esteem

The generation of self-esteem[2] as a basic exercise in the development of children and teenagers (Silbereisen & Kastner, 1978) is achieved to a large degree by recognizing one's own competence in sport. A good feeling of self-esteem in sport (or specifically in swimming), loosely interpreting the results of Brettschneider & Brandl-Bredenbeck (1997: 186f), leads one to see that there are quite positive influences in other areas of one's alter-ego.

Learning to swim, that is to say starting out into a new environment, should be managed by the instructor, taking into account the aspects mentioned above, so that the development of a high level of self-esteem is made possible.

1.7 The Ideal Age for Learning to Swim

"Water can survive without fish, but no fish can survive without water."

(Chinese Proverb)

At what age can children start learning to swim? What is the best age for laying the foundations for the first swimming techniques? When can children learn to swim in a group as well? This chapter will answer these questions. The following age groups will be considered:

- swimming for babies
- swimming for toddlers (age 1-3)
- swimming for pre-school children (age 4-5)
- swimming for school-age children (age 5-6)
- swimming for older school children (age 6-8)

---

[2]Self-esteem: cognitive evaluation of an appropriate part of one's ego concept.

Basically, learning to swim is possible at any age. The following reasons justify starting as early as possible:

- Swimming and playing in the water are very important for the health:
  - the muscular and cardiovascular systems are exercised
  - a good posture avoids damage and weaknesses later on
- Swimming is of educational and developmental psychological significance:
  - the child experiences pleasure in movement, playing games and sport
  - development of the personality
  - security and self-confidence
  - social behavior
- Learning to swim at an early age makes way to take up a good and worthwhile leisure activity

Swimming for Infants

By relying on the baby's reflex motor system, it is possible for infants to start to learn to swim as early as 6-8 weeks old. Prenatal reflexes are still active in the first few months of the child's life, and this make being in the water and moving around easier. The throat-closing reflex prevents the child from swallowing water (see Chapter 1.1).

After 4-6 months, the child's own will and ego takes over from the reflex motor system as it matures, and this is the time to start a swimming course. Swimming as a baby is generally seen as being positive.

It gives a positive **child-parent relationship**. Swimming together with their babies, fathers or mothers can enjoy valuable experiences, and learn just what their child can already do in the medium of water. The child undergoes a **variety of movement and development stimuli**. It has many **motor experiences**, which, at this age, it can not yet perform on land. The child and its motor skills develop more quickly and further than other children. This applies especially to the development of its coordination skills. Swimming also has a positive influence on the development of the posture and the cardiovascular system, and, moreover, the breathing organs become more efficient.

On the **emotional-affective** psychological side, through their pleasure at being able to move cleverly in the water, children demonstrate well-adjusted behavior. At the same time, the lower water temperature, compared to bath water, also toughens the children up. They have **social experiences** by meeting other children while swimming or simply by being independent of their parents in the water. Of course when babies learn to swim they are not going to be learning competitive swimming techniques such as the crawl or breaststroke. The emphasis is on their fundamental experience with water. Babies, helped by their parents, can learn to float on their backs, do elementary underwater diving and find out how to propel themselves forward by paddling with their legs. Swimming for babies, however, must also contain a few basic additional things. An adjustable raised floor in the pool allows the parents to be able to play and swim at an ideal depth (about 1.3 m, or just over four feet) with their children.

The children should already be prepared for the water at home by being changed over from the "baby bath" to going in the big bath tub with their parents and gradually getting used to a lower water temperature. Ear, nose and throat specialists criticize swimming for babies, because they state that 'swim babies' are more susceptible to ENT complaints. Other disadvantages might be:

- the water temperature (32°C/86°F)
- a relatively small group for an instructor or a coach
- facilities for diaper changing are rarely available

Should external conditions be acceptable, many of these points favor learning to swim while still a baby.

Swimming for Toddlers (Ages 1-3)
In this age group a few conditions in swimming for babies apply here as well. For example children can be taught initially with the assistance of a contact person (mother, father, uncle or aunt).

Since these children also chill fairly quickly, the water temperature must be at least 30°-32°C/80°-86°F. Learning competitive swimming techniques for this particular group is not a priority yet. The emphasis lies more on experiencing a variety of basic activities such as underwater diving, gliding, floating and jumping in, and those first experiences in movement which are aimed more at elementary or individual swimming techniques. After many years of experience with these target groups, I am able to present the following way to learn to swim on one's own:

- games that overcome fear and allow one to enjoy moving in the water (see Chapter 2.1)
- adopting positions on the water, either on the back or on the stomach, with the help of the parents, by:
  - pulling the child through the water; the child is right next to the person doing the pulling, with its head resting on the shoulder
  - pulling the child along by grasping under the armpits with outstretched arms
  - pulling the child along on its stomach
  - pulling the child along with a swimming bar
  - pulling the child along with a swimming board
  - while being pulled along, the child does paddling kicks with its legs; which can be "intensified" by wearing flippers
- dropping off any helper assistance by:
  - the helper pulls the child along in its wake
  - the helper pulls the child along and then lets it glide by itself using a swimming bar or swimming board
  - as above, but without the swimming bar or swimming board
- elementary movement in a forward direction:
  - "paddling" on its own with a swimming bar and flippers
  - "paddling" on its own with a swimming board and flippers
  - "paddling" on its own with flippers on the stomach or on the back
  - "paddling" on its own without flippers on the stomach or on the back

This is added to by experiences in underwater diving, jumping in, breathing, floating etc. Using this methodical system, described in more detail in Chapter 2, the children learn to swim by themselves as early as 2-3 years of age.

Swimming at Pre-School Age (Ages 4-5)

Children, aged 4-5 years, make rapid progress in their physical and motor development. The typical shape of their bodies at this age changes. The muscles become more developed and the circulatory system becomes more efficient. The children's vocabulary increases, which enables them to understand and carry out the instructor's commands better. This makes group instruction possible, while taking care that the groups don't get too big.

Based on the skills learned in swimming for beginners (underwater diving, breathing, jumping in, floating, gliding and making elementary movements), the way through to learning the basics of the crawl and backstroke can be put in place. The rhythmical two-arm techniques of the breaststroke and the butterfly stroke can also be worked on.

By developing the exercises, e.g., starting the butterfly stroke after jumping or diving in, the technique can be worked on or, better still, used as a playing activity. Children in this age group will not only just learn to enter the water by jumping off the ladder through a tire floating on the water, they may learn how to do it by diving in headfirst. Some children have been able to learn the butterfly stroke movement by means of the following additional exercise. "Jump headfirst from the third step of the pool ladder, through the first tire and come to the surface through the second tire, which is put behind the first". When the butterfly stroke action is intensified by use of flippers, they will have learned the basic movements of the butterfly stroke.

Swimming at School Age (Ages 5-6)
According to Lewin, children in this age group are at an ideal stage to learn to swim relative to their biological, motor, psychological and social skills (see Lewin, 1975: 20-22).

With regard to their motor development, the ability to learn new techniques is very marked. Instructions for motor actions can be carried out without any problems. Social behavior has developed to the stage where mutual respect permits group instruction and they can play together according to rules. Their ability to put up with psychological stress has increased, so that praise and rebukes and, hence, correction, are recognized as reasonable. For this reason, children in this and the next age group (ages 6-8) are considered to be at an ideal age to learn to swim.

Swimming for Older School Children (Ages 6-8)
The same arguments given in respect of school age children (ages 5-6) apply here also for the children in this group without any restriction. For this reason, swimming instruction at primary level should start in the first two years of school.

Conclusion

Learning to swim is possible at any age. The ideal learning age is school age (5-6 years) or 6-7 years at the latest. It is a good idea to become acquainted with water in a positive way as early as possible. The swimming instructor's problems consist of being able to be fair, when helping children with various physical abilities who are learning to swim, and get them all to achieve appropriate success according to their individual abilities. The type of activity ranges from getting used to the water to helping them learn various swimming techniques.

1.8   Choosing the First Stroke

"It is like playing the piano or riding a bicycle. Practice makes perfect."

(D. Lessing, 1979)

At this point, the arguments are brought together, in order to give an overview of what each of the strokes (crawl, backstroke or breaststroke) has, which speaks for it being the first technique to learn after the beginners swimming phase. Then, based on my own experience with various groups, I will offer a suggestion for the sequence, in which the techniques should be introduced. As teachers and instructors will see these arguments in a different light, every reader is free to take a different decision. However, when giving swimming instruction in school, a teacher should make his decision in favor of one type of swimming stroke or the other after weighing up the various arguments, and not because breaststroke was the first stroke his grandfather learned.

Up until 1925, the year when Wiessner's textbook "Teaching Swimming the Natural Way" was published, it was conventional in German-speaking countries to teach the breaststroke as the first technique (cf., Wilke, 1976: 14). The reasons for this go back to the historically rooted method called 'fishing' (Gutsmuth, 1978) and the method of General Von Pfuel, who taught breaststroke by numbers ("one, two, three"). After intensive beginner training Wiessner recommends the crawl or the breaststroke. Especially in the USA, Australia, former East Germany and the former Soviet Union the crawl was taught as the beginner's technique.

→ The following reasons **support the crawl** as the first technique to be learned in swimming:

Theoretical Reasons
* The crawl is associated with familiar coordinated patterns that the child has learned while running, walking and crawling.
* The sequences of movements in the crawl run along the length of the body, so that a better feeling and control of movement is achieved.

Psychological and Methodological Reasons
* The crawl satisfies the child's urge to move, especially with its enthusiastic, lively movements, because its arms and legs are moving all the time.
* Following gliding, as one of the learning goals of beginner swimming, the distance covered can be slightly lengthened by using the crawl leg kick. This quickly leads to being able to swim on one's own.
* The leg strokes are easier to learn than those in the breaststroke.
* The coordination of the arm and leg movements can be achieved without any problem in the crawl.
* The basic form of the crawl can be learned quickly, so that the swimming experience, e.g., swimming alone across the width of the pool, can be achieved early on.
* The first swimming award can be fairly quickly achieved using the crawl.

Motivational Reasons
* As the crawl is the fastest swimming stroke, it is also the most attractive for children.
* The children can also use flippers. Using them, children experience swimming on their own and forward movement much earlier than by using the breaststroke; they are also able to experience the speed at which they can move through the water because of the greater power from the flippers.
* The majority of swimming competitions in regional, national and international championships are carried out using the crawl, enabling more competitors to win "medals" (Marc SPITZ won seven Gold Medals at the 1972 Olympic Games).

Medical Reasons

- The crawl relaxes the area of the spine, because the alternating arm movement in each phase produces more forward movement than the leg strokes do, thus stretching the spine.
- Mobility in the area of the shoulders also has a positive effect.
- Less strain is placed on the knees joint and cartilage.
- The alternating arm movements give a better posture.

Reasons Related to Body Movement

- Training in the crawl provides the basis for movement-related techniques of the backstroke and the butterfly stroke.

Uses of the Crawl

- The crawl provides the basic stroke in water polo, synchronized swimming and diving.
- Long-distance swimmers, e.g., triathlon swimmers and 1500-meter swimmers etc., prefer the crawl, as this is a more economic technique.

Disadvantages of the Crawl

- Breathing is harder and is also difficult to learn.
- It is difficult to keep one's bearings in the water.
- As long as the swimmer cannot master this stroke perfectly, he swims in an overly cramped manner or expends too much physical effort, which leads to rapid fatigue. For this reason, stamina in swimming is difficult for beginners.

→ **The backstroke** sees almost all the same arguments as for the crawl speaking for it, with the exception of adding the following:
- it is the fastest stroke
- it is used in most swimming competitions
- it is used in long-distance swimming

Additional positive points for the backstroke crawl:
- unimpaired breathing
- the ability to visually control the leg movements

The following points count against the Backstroke Crawl:

- it is difficult to control direction when swimming on one's back

- the stretched-out position on the back is difficult for nervous children to assume

→ **The breaststroke** has the following points going for it as a beginner's stroke:

Analytical Movement Reasons
- It is easier to retain visual and aural orientation than when doing the crawl.
- It is easier to breathe, as the head stays above water.
- The symmetrical movements enable smoother movements in the water.
- The gliding phase enables the swimmer to concentrate on the movements that follow.
- Fatigue does not occur so quickly.
- There is greater hydrostatic buoyancy, as all four limbs are under water.

Motivation Reasons:
- The stamina required for having to stay longer on top of the water, lasts longer.

Uses
- It is particularly important for life saving.
- It opens up the field of diving.

Disadvantages of the breaststroke are almost all the same as those listed for the crawl.

All the advantages of the breaststroke and the crawl are set out in the table.

Advantages of the Crawl	Advantages of the Breaststroke
• Familiar pattern, with crossed alternate coordination	• Symmetrical movements
• Movements are close to the body	• Gliding phase
• Easier to follow on with gliding	• No fatigue
• The leg kick is easier	• Good orientation
• Easier coordination	• Breathing is easier
• Children's urge to move	• Greater buoyancy
• Quick to learn	• The swimmer is on top of the water longer
• Fastest stroke technique	• Used in life saving and underwater diving
• Flippers usable	
• Majority of swimming competitions	
• Easy on the spine	
• Mobility	
• Easy on the knees	
• Good posture	
• Related movement sequence	
• Used in water polo, synchronized swimming, and diving	
• Long-distance swimming	

Figure 12: *Choice of the First Swimming Strokes*

There are advantages and disadvantages for all three types of swimming stroke, which can be introduced after the swimmers have got used to the water. Depending on the type of group or aims of the swimming instruction, the arguments for and against can be seen differently. Thus, for elderly people it is certainly more important to be able to keep their heads above water, and see where they are swimming. For younger children, on the other hand, other arguments come to the fore that make the crawl the first type of stroke they favor. But there are also different aims that can influence the decision in favor of one stroke or another. This is why instructors of the DRLG (German Life Saving Association) teach breaststroke as the first stroke, because they are primarily concerned with swimming for rescue purposes.

For pre-schoolers and primary school children, I recommend starting with the alternate stroke techniques of the crawl or the backstroke for educational, psychological and methodical reasons. The familiar pattern (crossed coordination), the easy transition to gliding, the opportunity to use flippers, the easier leg kick movements and coordination, the children's urge to do movement, and medical consideration are all factors, which make the decision in favor of the crawl the right one for this target group. Here, learning processes can often take place parallel to the crawl or the backstroke. Following on from gliding, the use of leg kicking strokes, while on the back or the stomach, make it possible to lengthen the distance glided. For this reason, the crawl and the backstroke can become the first or second stroke the swimmers learn. When the children have gained confidence in both of these techniques, they can also learn the more difficult breaststroke relatively quickly.

With older people, we often come across the view that swimming means the breaststroke. These ideas are sometimes so deeply anchored that people cannot be talked into learning the crawl. In particular, elderly people with back problems would be better advised to begin with the backstroke.

Handicapped people often learn to swim on their own via the backstroke. Of course this must be decided very much on an individual basis. This is because every form and the actual degree of handicap can have such great differences that it is impossible to give general advice. Particularly with handicaps, where it is difficult to control the head movements, e.g., spastics, lying on the back, it is sometimes the only way to move independently without swimming aids.

With many forms of handicap, a unilateral orientation to standardized swimming techniques is not advisable. It is a question more that an individual technique must be found, dependent on the movements possible by that person. For example, this can be an alternate leg movement technique while on the back using flippers.

So that children learn the various ways that there are of moving through the water so that they do not get fixed on one technique, the swimming instruction should be constructed so that they can try out a number of ways of moving through the water while they are still "non-swimmers". This varied method of instruction (see Gildenhard, 1977) makes it also possible, based on the many different movement actions, to learn several swimming techniques.

1.9 Games and Exercise Equipment Used in Teaching Swimming

"You often have to play the fiddle the way it wants to be played."

(German Proverb)

In the literature on swimming for beginners (Lewin, 1994; Wilke, 1976, 1992; Durlach, 1994, Volck, 1977) various equipment is introduced, which makes games and exercises in the water more interesting and varied for beginners. These aids are divided into various categories. I will divide them into two groups; static and movable aids. The static aids and practice equipment are divided further into toys, floating (bouyancy) aids and movement aids according to the use to which they can be put.

1.9.1 Static Equipment

The static aids include objects built into the swimming pool such as the edge of the pool, the overflow channel, the ladder and the steps. They are particularly suitable to support the body floating by enabling the swimmer to hold on to the side of the pool or support himself on the steps, for example. These aids can also be used to practice partial movements of complete swimming strokes. For example, kicking the legs for the crawl can be done while supporting oneself on the steps. But they can also be helpful in other areas of swimming for beginners. By performing small leaps from the steps, with and without assistance, the swimmers can be prepared for jumping in and diving into the water from the edge of the pool (see Chapter 2.4). The starting block, the 1 or 3-meter high-diving board right up to the 10 m diving tower are also static and exercise aids. Even lane dividers in the pool can be used as static aids.

1.9.2   Movable Equipment

Play Equipment

The use of play equipment is particularly important in swimming for beginners. They can help distract nervous children, who are scared of water and emphasize the fun in being in and playing in the water. Play equipment makes exercises, representing steps towards learning goals in swimming for beginners, more interesting and divert the swimmer's attention from the idea that they are "just practicing" and let the children get to grips with the water and the equipment in a "fun" way.

In the following paragraphs I will describe a few of the play equipment aids. I will not list them all; rather, I will mention them in the context of the aims and content of beginner swimming in which they are presented as examples. Interesting play equipment is not the primary criterion for designing swimming instruction for beginners. The aims of swimming for beginners should determine the instructional content and the methods, and these, in turn, should determine the choice of the game and exercise equipment.

The idea of **"getting used to the water by playing"**, with its partial learning aim of having fun and pleasure in and moving about in the water, makes the use of play equipment very suitable. Thus, any children's play equipment that floats (such as ducks, balls, balloons and other objects) can be included. Music and children's songs and dancing are also part of the repertoire, which help children overcome their fear of water and lets them enjoy being in it.

The partial learning aims in **"underwater diving"** can be designed so that they are more interesting with the use of the following equipment: objects such as diving rings, diving stones, "treasures" , made by using old objects such as spoons, cooking pots, boxes etc., can all act as incentives for the swimmers to dive beneath the surface of the water. Stones wrapped in aluminum foil can also be used suitably.

Breathing techniques can be practiced by various games where play equipment such as *table tennis balls, little boats, soap dishes* and *balls* etc., can be used.

Jumping in and diving can be made more attractive by the use of the following play equipment:

* *a rope*, held high enough to be within arm's length, and to which various objects can be attached and then retrieved, such as balloons, sweets etc
* *tires* that the swimmers can jump into
* *bars, swimming boards, mats and inflatable mattresses* which the swimmers can either jump over or into etc

For **gliding** and **floating**, the following play and exercise equipment can be used to support partial aims: *swimming bars, swimming boards, buoys, underwater balls, other balls, mats.*

In order to assist with the **elementary movements** in the water up to doing the first swimming strokes the following equipment can be used:

* *swimming bars:* even small children and handicapped children can use this equipment in order to learn to stop "clinging" to carers or parents and glide and move about on their own in the water.
* *flippers:* flippers can help even very small children (aged 1-2) and those children with handicaps such as quadriplegics, whose means of propulsion is very limited, to learn to swim on their own using paddling movements.
* *swimming boards, pull-buoys:* these aids enable the swimmer to concentrate on the movement of the arms and legs. For this reason they can learn to swim using natural movements they have already learned.

For **games using balls** there are various forms and types of balls: balloons, "slow motion" balls, water polo balls, rugby balls, underwater balls etc. These can be used to play familiar catching and throwing games, relays etc., and the bigger ball games: water polo, water basket ball, water volleyball, water soccer, water biathlons, underwater ball, underwater rugby.

Life saving provides a repertoire of exercise and games equipment that can be used in swimming for beginners and for swimming instruction for advanced students: *t-shirts, clothing, flippers, rescue lines* etc. Relay games in which the swimmers have to take off or put on clothing are especially popular and simultaneously improve the children's feeling of safety in the water.

Scuba diving equipment (flippers, goggles and snorkels) can be used for a variety of **diving** games. "Sandwich" diving, "hunting for treasure", marathon relays etc., are only a few of the possibilities.

The use of play equipment in **water gymnastics** as a means of entertainment and relaxation is discussed fully in the literature on this subject (see Beigeluhl & Brinckmann, 1989; Ott & Schmidt, 1995; Zeitvogel, 1992). The following equipment is especially suitable for loosening up water gymnastics and making it more interesting: *water dumbbells, swimming boards, pull-buoys, paddles, gloves, balls of all sorts, aqua-jogging vests* etc.

Floating Aids

Floating aids have almost always been used for beginner swimming. In ancient times and in the Middle Ages, *belts made of rushes, inflatable pig's bladders* inter alia were used as aids to support beginners in the water.

Today we take "floating aids" to mean those aids that can be attached to the body and which help the swimmer stay on the surface. Such aids include *inflatable arm bands, inflatable swimming 'eggs', water-wings* and the like. The **advantages** of these aids are that they help to give nervous children a feeling of safety. At the same time they can gradually learn to do without the assistance of helpers (parents or instructors) and move around in the water on their own. By using water wings in particular, children can easily change from floating on their stomachs to lying on their backs.

However, the **disadvantages** outweigh the advantages, so that since the publication of the book "Instruction in Natural Swimming" by Kurt Wiessner (1925), almost all swimming methods for beginners do without these aids.

A particular disadvantage is the distortion of the floating effect of the swimmer's own body. It is precisely the fact that the swimmer's own body should experience the buoyant, floating effect and the fact that the swimmer can stay on the surface without using much energy is the actual moment of realization that leads to a secure feeling while swimming. If buoyancy aids are used this experience is only deferred. Floating is ascribed to the water wings or the other inflatable swimming aids. Discarding these aids later on leads rather to greater insecurity than having to get to grips with the water without them right from the start.

The swimming position is also worsened by these aids. "Water-wing-children" can be recognized by their almost vertical position in the water, which makes rapid progress in water impossible.

In addition, the movements learned in the vertical position are different to those learned in the horizontal position. This requires a re-learning process. Inflatable arm bands also restrict the child's ability to move in the water similarly.

Movement Aids

The classical movement aids are *swimming boards* and *pull-buoys*. In contrast to the classical buoyancy aids they do not detract from the swimmer's floating experience, as they are not attached to the body. They support the floating effect only so far that the beginner can concentrate fully on carrying out movements such as the over-arm movement of the crawl or the leg movement in the breaststroke. In this way they assist the learning process in swimming.

Other aids to movement are *swimming bars, flippers and paddles*. The bar is used especially with beginners and gives nervous children a greater feeling of security during gliding on their own than the swimming board, which can tip to one side.

The swimming bar is also a piece of games equipment which can be used for various games and exercises.

Flippers are suitable both for beginners as well as advanced swimmers. In particular, they increase speed with only slight leg movements needed. Thus handicapped children, with minimum movement ability, are able learn to swim on their own. Learning the crawl, backstroke crawl and the butterfly breaststroke are also made a lot easier when the swimmer uses flippers.

The paddles are used more for swimmers who have already mastered swimming techniques to some extent. These techniques can be improved with the help of the paddles or allow specific training aims such as stamina training to be made easier.

1.10   Organizing Swimming Instruction

"Do not rebuke the river if you fall into the water."

(Korean Saying)

Is Swimming a Dangerous Sport?
Swimming can be categorized as one of the less dangerous sports, being low down in the list of the accident statistics behind other sports. In Germany, only 4% of school sports accidents can be attributed to swimming (cf. Landesinstitut für Schule und Weiterbildung (The (German) Institute for State Schools and Further Education, 1993: 7).

But the fact that many people categorize swimming as dangerous is probably due to the fact that they are very afraid of drowning and that there have been a few serious accidents. Headlines in German newspapers such as "Drowned in the lake" (Neue Westfälische, 1977) give a negative impression.

If the regulations pertaining to care and supervision are adhered to, swimming is a safe sport that opens up many opportunities for movement. It is quite properly called a healthy sport, since it offers practically every age group, right up to the very elderly, the opportunity to do something for one's health and physical condition. For example, it is still possible even when the knees are so damaged that jogging and walking as exercises are no longer possible.

Letter to parents (example)

(The school's address)   Date

Dear Parent or Guardian,

Your son/daughter .... will be taking part in swimming lessons during this school year. Please let us know whether there any special considerations or medical circumstances, which will have to be taken into consideration if your child takes part in swimming, diving or jumping activities.

Please supply a doctor's medical certificate attesting to any health problems that might preclude participation in swimming lessons.

Please fill in, sign and return the lower part of this letter to the school by ....(date).

....
(Class teacher)   (Sports teacher)

Please separate here

- ✂

....
(First and last name of the child)

(Please tick where appropriate)

1. ☐ There are no health problems preventing participation in swimming lessons.

2. ☐ My/Our child may take part in swimming lessons, but has the following health problems:
....

3. ☐ My/Our child may not take part in swimming lessons for health reasons. (A doctor's medical certificate is attached.)

....
Place/Date   (Signature of parent or guardian)

A parents' evening may supplement this letter or possibly replace it. If a child supplies a doctor's medical certificate for an extended period of time, it is advisable to talk to the parents about the reason for the child's exemption from swimming.

Before the First Swimming Lessons

Information for Parents
Before the first lessons, parents should be informed by letter that their children will be taking part in swimming lessons in the kindergarten, school (e.g., in sports instruction in Year 1), or at the swimming club. This letter should contain a section to be filled in, signed and returned by the parents. In the letter the parents state that they consent to their child taking part in swimming lessons and confirm that they have no contagious diseases or other illnesses that might preclude the child's participation in swimming lessons.

Exemption from Swimming
Some illnesses, allergies, or possibly even types of handicap may make exemption from swimming instruction necessary. Ear problems (ear-drum, inner ear), a chlorine allergy, skin problems etc., can lead to exemption from swimming lessons. With the following illnesses or forms of handicap it is appropriate to decide in individual cases whether the child concerned ought to take part in full swimming lessons, partially or perhaps not at all:

- cardiovascular damage
- diabetes, astma
- fits
- cerebrally-based motor disturbances etc.

In many cases, the practice of having a "three-party discussion" with the parents and/or the child concerned, the swimming instructor and the child's doctor has proved its worth. Swimming instruction is particularly well suited to integrate handicapped children (see Chapter 1.4). For this reason parents, instructors, handicapped and non-handicapped children should also make use of these opportunities.

Rules for Behavior in the Swimming Pool

Swimming Attire
It is recommended that the parents be informed either orally or in writing as to which "paraphernalia" the children should bring to a swimming lesson:

- swimming togs
- towel
- shower shampoo or soap, to wash the body before swimming

- bathing sandals in order to avoid infection (e.g. athlete's foot)
- a hair-dryer, particularly in the cold season (sometimes a second towel will suffice to dry the hair)
- a cap or other head covering in order to protect against colds or similar illnesses after swimming

It goes without saying that the person in charge should always wear swimming attire in order to be able to jump into the water to save someone.

Swimming Pool Rules

Before the first visit to the swimming pool, the children must be made aware of the type of behavior required at the pool, the rules of swimming and rules for the swimming pool premises. As a copy of the swimming pool regulations are normally available from the city or pool authorities, these should be passed on at least in abbreviated form to the children. Swimming pool regulations in Germany are worked out between those swimming clubs that carry out training for competitive swimming – the DLRG (Deutsche Lebens-Rettungs-Gesellschaft e.V. (German Life Saving Association)), the DSV (Deutscher Schwimmverband e.V., (the German Swimming Association)), the DRK (Deutsches Rotes Kreuz (German Red Cross)), the DTB (Deutscher Turner-Bund (German Gymnastics Association)), the VDST (Verband Deutscher Sporttaucher e.V. (German Scuba Diving Association)) – and the Ministries of Education in each State (Kultusministerien der Laender) in Germany. All these organizations are mentioned in shortened form on the certificates accompanying swimming awards.

Swimming Rules

- Make yourself familiar with the rules on self-help in the water for unexpected situations such as cramp, eddies, currents etc.
- Never go swimming on a completely full or empty stomach.
- Cool down before you go into the water and get out of the water immediately you start to freeze.
- If a non-swimmer, only go chest-deep into the water.
- Jump into the water only if it is deep enough beneath you and free from obstacles.
- Unfamiliar river-banks can conceal hazards.

- Avoid swampy or overgrown waters.
- Shipping routes, breakwaters, locks, bridge-piers, and weirs are not swimming areas.
- Swimming is dangerous to life during a storm.
- Do not overestimate your strength and ability in open waters.
- Inflatable mattresses, old tire inner tubes and rubber animals are dangerous playthings in the water.
- There are special hazards in swimming at the seaside beach: ask the locals before going into the water.
- Have consideration for others in the water, especially children.
- Do not foul the water – behave in a hygienic fashion.
- After coming out of the water, change out of your swimming attire and dry off.
- Don't spend too long in the sun when sunbathing.
- Never call for help if you are not in danger, but render aid to others if required.

Special aspects of danger must also be noted:
- Running along the wet ground beside the pool (especially if it is tiled) is not allowed.

It is also forbidden to:
- Push people into the water.
- Scream for help when not in danger etc.

It is not enough for the swimming instructor to point out the rules once; he must also ensure that they are adhered to.

The First Visit to the Swimming Pool
When a group first visits the swimming pool, all the facilities should be pointed out and the whole premises shown and explained to the visitors:
- the changing areas
- the shower facilities
- the non-swimmers pool
- the swimming and (if appropriate) the diving areas
- the sauna and any other additional facilities

Where May Swimming Be Taught?

Generally, swimming cannot be taught in just any swimming pool, as a few safety regulations must be adhered to. For this reason swimming instruction in German schools, for example, may only be given in pools supervised by somebody with a State approved life saving certificate. This guarantees that safety measures are in accordance with the regulations and that the chlorine levels are constantly checked. In Germany, private pools may also therefore only be used for swimming instruction if a State Examined Swimming Master is in charge. The reader should check with the authorities to see what the requirements are in his particular country.

Who May Teach Swimming?

Teaching swimming in schools may only be carried out by someone who is able to prove that they have been trained in life saving. This rule is also supposed to apply to instruction out of school hours. As an example of the restrictions prevalent in Germany, the standard of life saving is laid down as follows by the Ministry of Education in the State North Rhine-Westphalia:

- Starting from the surface of the water the candidate must be able to fetch an object weighing about 5 kg from the bottom of the pool, i.e., from a depth of 2 to 3 m, and bring it to the side of the pool.
- Be able to dive to a depth of approx 10 m.
- Be able to prevent a person being rescued from clinging on to the rescuer or be able to disengage oneself from such a person.
- Be able to drag a person of approximately the same weight by the head or the under the arms for a distance of 15 m and bring this person on to dry land;
- and, be able to **take immediate action to save a life.**

(see Landesinstitut für Schule und Weiterbildung (the German Institute for State Schools and Further Education), 1993: 117).
This life saving ability is the prerequisite for being able to supervise school pupils when swimming and teaching swimming in all types of pools.

In Germany, the ability to perform life saving must be documented by the relevant local Board of Education, the DLRG (German Life Saving Association), the DRK (German Red Cross) or an approved institution of further education of instructors. It seems fair that the trained swimmer should have to refresh his life saving skills, especially his emergency skills, by attending further swimming education classes, so that he can apply these immediately in the event of an emergency.

Size of the Group and Supervision

Any group of pre-school beginners should be small and all members should be manageable and be able to be seen at a glance. In this way the instructor can devote time to individual needs and demands. This is possible with a group of 6-12 children; in exceptional cases (homogeneous groups) the group can also consist of up to 15 members. However, if the group is made up of nervous or handicapped children, it is advisable to have fewer numbers.

It is "normal" to have a non-homogeneous group of pupils, as children come to swimming lessons with:

- different abilities
- various previous motor experiences
- with no fears or with varying types of fear
- various physical abilities
- various degrees of willingness to learn, which ranges from learning-blocks to "over-motivation"
- various ages and stages of development
- abnormal movement actions
- various types of handicap or no handicap

For swimming instruction at school, the German State Ministries of Education have laid down differing regulations pertaining to the size of the group. For example in North Rhine-Westphalia, the older regulations stipulated a maximum of fifteen pupils in a group at primary school level.

In the latest instructions on this subject (29 March 1993) these regulations are somewhat less clear: "The size of the group in swimming instruction should, as a rule, correspond to the size of the class or course group, as laid down by the regulations pertaining to the level of the class and the type of school". (Germany's Institute for State Schools and Further Education 1993: 119).

Limiting the size of the class to 15 children is recommended only in special conditions: for example, if instruction for beginners can only be given under difficult conditions, e.g., the danger of slipping due to a sharp drop in the bottom of the pool between the non-swimmers and swimmers areas, or where two different groups are being taught at the same time, the groups should be limited to fifteen pupils.

The final decision as to the requirement for supervision is left to the school principal. The school authorities, together with the teachers concerned, make the decision as to the size of the group. For pupils at special schools and for teaching mixed groups in normal schools the size of the group is set "according to the relevant educational requirements".

Supervision
As in any sports instruction, the principle of one teacher being responsible per group of pupils also applies when teaching swimming. As a pool attendant is normally present at a pool, he can be called on to assist, but must be released from his general supervisory duties in and around the pool. If supervisory personnel have to take care of the public section of the pool, they cannot be involved in supervising school groups at the same time.

Parents or experienced older pupils can also be used to assist as well if they have life saving skills (for example, in Germany this equates to the life saving association's Bronze Medal), but such assistance does not relieve the instructors from their ultimate supervisory responsibility.

The supervising instructor must position himself so that he can see all the children in the water. He should not stay in the water with the pupils unless this is required for specific methods or instructional reasons.

If a group of swimmers and non-swimmers are being taught by only one instructor, instruction must take place in the learner's pool. The teacher must also check that all pupils are present before entering the pool premises, immediately upon getting out of the pool and before leaving the pool premises (– check the numbers three times!).

Special Demands on the Swimming Instructor
Individual Supervision is necessary in the following situations:

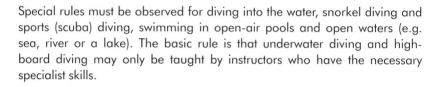

* pupils swimming in deep water for the first time
* swimming under water for extended distances
* deep underwater diving

Special rules must be observed for diving into the water, snorkel diving and sports (scuba) diving, swimming in open-air pools and open waters (e.g. sea, river or a lake). The basic rule is that underwater diving and high-board diving may only be taught by instructors who have the necessary specialist skills.

Diving
First of all, the diving board must be checked for safety. Diving is only permitted in the area of water that has been specially approved for this purpose. The diving area may be entered only when the water is clear. The instructor should make sure that the pupils dive only in a forward direction (with the exception of the backstrokes).

A minimum depth of water applies in the case of starting dives and rolling turns:

* starting dives and rolling turns: 1.8 m
* headfirst diving from the side of the pool: 2.5 m

Underwater Diving
This a popular sport, but a few safety aspects must be strictly adhered to. For this reason it is important for the instructor and the pupils to know about a few basic points that must be adhered to:

* the danger of "a swimming pool blackout" through hyperventilation
* blocked eardrums caused by overpressure
* injuries due to pressure when diving with goggles

For this reason the following rules should be followed:

* never dive alone
* dive only if you are in good health and you feel fit

- never dive wearing goggles
- keep an eye on your fellow divers
- don't dive if, when pressing your ears on land, you don't feel a definite pressure on your eardrum
- stop diving if shooting pains in your ears or your forehead/nose area set in

Swimming on Other Occasions
Swimming with pupils on other occasions, e.g. on school walks and other trips, should only be carried out in a public, supervised swimming pool. If, in individual cases, a non-supervised public pool is used, all pupils should have some form of bronze-level national swimming qualification. The supervisor should possess some form of national lifesaving qualification in silver and be acquainted with the conditions at the pool (see the German Institute for State Schools and Further Education 1993: 123).

1.11 Forms of Organization

"When two people embrace, a circle is formed."

(Hebbel)

1.11.1 General Considerations

The choice of the form of organization depends on various factors – the external conditions, such as the type of premises and the equipment available, the requirements of the group in question (size, level of ability, composition) and on the goals and content of the swimming instruction.

The Premises
The type of organization that can be planned depends on whether a learner's pool (with or without a rising floor), a pool for swimmers, a pool with a shallow and a deep end, a pool with additional diving areas is available, or only part of it has these facilities. Equally important for the choice of content are the types of available equipment: lane dividers, swimming boards, pull-buoys, balls, diving rings etc.

Target Groups

The choice of the type of organization depends also on the *size of the target group*. Especially with large learner groups, the form of organization that should be selected is the one that guarantees the best use of training intensity. Even the *age* and *ability* of the members of the group influences which form of organization is chosen. This means that children who have just learned a particular swimming technique can practice it by swimming across the width of the pool. They then correct and perfect it while swimming shorter stretches in the pool, and then practice it until it comes automatically and before they use it in longer distances such as full lengths of the pool.

The composition of the group can also influence the choice of content and form of organization. In heterogeneous groups, where people of various ages or physical ability are learning to swim, games involving the whole group must take the "smallest" members, and those who are not quite so capable, into consideration.

For example the depth, in pools with rising bottoms, must be adjusted for the body height of the smallest members of the group, ideas for games must be adjusted down to the ability of the weakest and the strain in various forms of exercises adjusted to the physical limits of the weaker members. In many cases it would be ideal to offer games and exercises in varying forms and standards of achievement to take account of this (cf. Teaching Theories, Chapter 1.4.2).

Goals and Content

The content of the swimming lesson and the form of organization are dependent on the aims. The aims determine the content, the content determines the form. For this reason, the aims of a swimming group should be formulated first of all. Consideration can be given later to which types of games and exercises best achieve these aims. Depending on the aims and content, the form of organization should be chosen that best suits the content, makes best use of the time available and guarantees learning success for everybody helping to achieve the aims set.

Aquafun – First Steps

1.11.2   Forms of Organization in a Learners' Pool

1. Forming a Circle

a) Forming a circle in the water
with the instructor
Making a circle, in which holding
hands with the instructor or a
partner provides additional security
is especially suitable for nervous
learners. The children needing the
most help or who are the most
nervous are allowed to make
physical contact with the instructor.

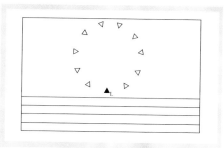

Figure 13: *Forming a circle with
the instructor*

b) Forming a circle, instructor
stays at the side of the pool
The pupils stand in a circle holding
hands or not. Both forms of
organization are suitable for
various forms of games and
exercises (see also Integration
through Games and Sports,
Rheker, 2000 for explanations of
the games listed):

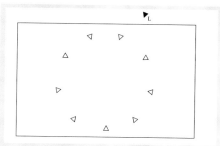

Figure 14: *Forming a circle with
the instructor standing on the side
of the pool*

- for getting used to the water in the form of a game: "Eeny-Miny-Mo"; "I
  sent a letter to my love"; "Ring a ring o'roses" etc.
- games to do with floating: carousel; paddling with the hands etc.
- games to do with breathing: blowing table-tennis balls along the surface
  of the water, blowing bubbles
- games to do with diving under the surface of the water: "washbowl",
  "diving through the legs in a circle" etc.

2. Group Dispersed around the Swimming Pool

Many types of games and exercises can make use of the group when dispersed:

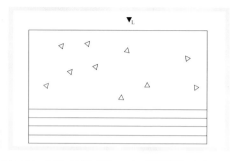

Figure 15: *A dispersed group in the swimming pool*

- communicative and interactive games: the "molecular game", the "welcome game", "hunter ball" etc.
- running and catching games such as chain catch, catching and freeing, the " Magic Mouse" etc.
- games with music
- diving, breathing, floating exercises etc., for partial learning goals.

3. Exercises on the Pool Steps

The pool steps are a very suitable "stepping-stone" towards many of the partial goals and the corresponding types of games and exercises. It is a good way to prepare for diving from the side of the pool:

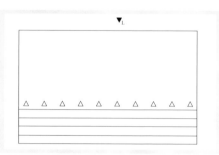

Figure 16: *Exercises on the steps*

- simple jumping in feet-first
- creative jumping: "Who can do the funniest jumps into the water?"
- diving in and gliding

Floating on the surface can be learnt with the aid of the steps:

- floating parts of the body
- backward and forward press-ups

Elementary kicking movements with the legs can be introduced on the steps.

Breathing can also be taught on the steps with the following exercises:

- in a forward press-up position breathing out slowly while in the water
- breathing in a rhythmic fashion

4. Swimming Widths and Lengths of the Learners' Pool

Simple games and exercises in forward movement in the water can be carried out width- or length-wise in the learners' pool:

- walking, running or jumping through the water
- races: e.g., with or without using the arms
- elementary arm movements whilst running
- gliding along with and without the help of a partner
- relay games, inter alia

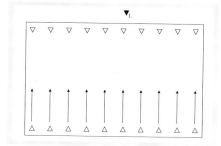

Figure 17: *Swimming across the width of the pool*

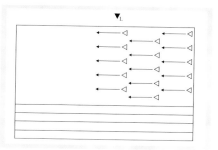

Figure 18: *Swimming the full length of the pool*

1.11.3   Forms of Organization in a Swimmers' Pool

1. Swimming the width of the pool

a) Forming groups for learning swimming stroke techniques
When the pupils are able to swim a width of the pool by using a swimming stroke they have just learned, the following arrangement is appropriate:

Figure 19: *Swimming a width of the pool*

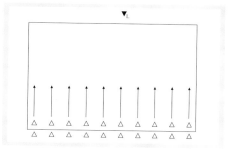

The following techniques can be learned in arrangements like this:

- gliding
- kicking movements with the legs with or without swimming boards
- arm strokes with or without pull-buoys
- coordination of legs and arms
- sprint exercises
- diving

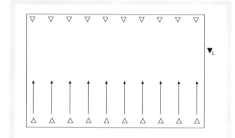

Figure 20: *Swimming a width of the pool*

b) Exercises to improve swimming techniques
In order to learn swimming techniques in a controlled situation, (arm strokes, leg kicking movements) these can be improved by the following forms of organization, whereby a partner can be used to watch and correct the movements:

Learner A swims towards B, who watches and checks A, who swims back, trying to use the correct form. Then B swims towards A, who now corrects B, etc.

c) Swimming in waves
Three or more groups swim, one after another, in waves across the width of the pool e.g., to practice or reinforce swimming techniques or partial swimming techniques.

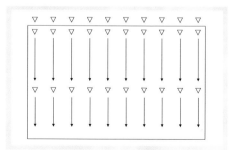

Figure 21: *Swimming in waves*

d) Secure edge of the pool

When practicing backstroke techniques, it is important that learners do not become anxious that they will swim against the edge of the pool. They will only be able to swim across the whole width of the pool if they do the crawl backstroke without feeling scared.

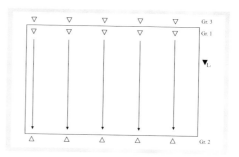

Figure 22: *Secure edge of the pool*

If the learners get afraid, e.g., of swimming against the edge of the pool, they will often lose their correct position in the middle of the width by turning the head down onto the chest or by looking behind them. So in order to practice the crawl backstroke technique, it is advisable to use three groups. First, Group 1 swims towards Group 2, which makes sure that nobody swims against the edge of the pool. Group 2 then swims towards Group 3. Finally, Group 3 swims towards Group 1, which then secures the edge of the pool so that nobody swims against the edge of it.

2. Swimming the Full Length of the Pool

As soon as learners are able to swim the width of the pool more than once, the pupils can be formed into the following groups for swimming the full length of the pool.

a) Swimming the full length of the pool

When each swimmer has swum one whole lane they walk back along the edge of the pool. The following groups can be formed:

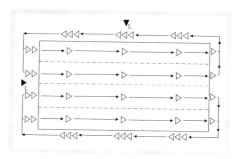

Figure 23: *Swimming the full length of the pool*

- when learners swim the full length of the pool for the first time, or
- when they are practicing kicking or arm movements
- for special training of the breathing rhythm (breathing after every 3, 5 & 10 strokes)
- when practicing starts
- when practicing the breaststroke after diving into the pool
- when swimming underwater for a short distance and then swimming further
- when spurt swimming

b) Swimming more than one full length of the pool

When the learners are able to swim more than one full length of the pool, the arrangement shown in Figures 24 and 25 can be used. This type of organization is especially suitable for the following possible applications:

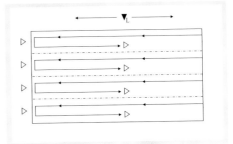

Figure 24: *Swimming more than one full length of the pool*

- warming up in the water
- practicing arm strokes or kicking
- teaching the finer points of swimming techniques
- reinforcing and consolidating swimming techniques
- practicing basic stamina
- practicing exercise forms of interval training
- practicing coordination
- cooling down in the water

c) Extended swimming training
For its uses see 2b above

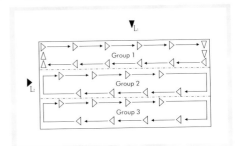

Figure 25: *Extended swimming training*

3. Other types of organization

Completely different types of organized arrangements can be chosen to liven up the lessons and to make instruction and training more interesting and varied. The instructor can well make use of his imagination when applying any variation. As one example from a wide range of options, I would like to mention the N-Form:

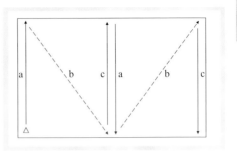

Figure 26: *Further forms of organization*

In the N-Form, lanes in the width of the pool are combined with diagonal ones. For example, Lane A can be used for the crawl kick, Lane B for swimming the full crawl, and Lane C for the crawl arm stroke. But other swimming techniques can also practiced as a combination or different techniques introduced in order to train coordination, e.g., the crawl arm stroke with the butterfly leg kick, underwater swimming strokes, rotation swimming (at every stroke the swimmer turns from a stomach position onto his back) etc.

II PRACTICAL SWIMMING FOR BEGINNERS

2 The Various Areas and Goals of Swimming for Beginners

"Everybody just wants to send their head to school on its own, but the whole human being always comes too."

(Ursula Förster)

Literature on swimming instruction lists different sub-areas or partial learning goals in the area of swimming for beginners. Kurt Wiessner (1925), on whose methods all modern methods of swimming for beginners are based, names the following goals for the part of instruction which takes place before learning the actual swimming techniques:

- immersing the head
- partial floating
- free floating
- gliding

The very successful book, written by Gerhard Lewin (1975), "Schwimmen mit kleinen Leuten" ("Swimming with young people"), which was revised in 1994 and re-titled "Schwimmen kinderleicht" ("Swimming is Child's Play"), notes the following partial learning goals for swimming for beginners:

- diving underwater
- jumping in and diving
- gliding
- moving forwards
- breathing

Kurt Wilke (1979), who gained world-wide acknowledgement for his methodical revision and approach to the subject of swimming, divides the methodology of beginners swimming beginners into the following partial learning goals: diving underwater, jumping in and diving, breathing, floating, gliding. Games and exercises for getting used to the water also come in to have their own importance. No methodology for beginners swimming can ignore these fundamental principles. Before an instructor can develop his own ideas based on these proved methods, I would like to mention some basic thoughts on teaching methods and learning in swimming lessons. Many methods of teaching swimming for beginners are influenced by the goal of introducing learners to competitive swimming techniques as soon as possible.

This teaching at an early stage of only a few techniques (four Olympic swimming techniques) very quickly restricts the versatility of the possible movements by, in, and under the water, thus restricting the ways in which children develop and doesn't allow them to be fully used.

The rash teaching of the specific, sequential movements, such as those required in swimming techniques, is more of a hindrance than a help "in revealing functional movements and in the development of different patterns of perception and action, and it prevents the experience of movement and the development of feeling for movement from being gained" (Loibl, 1992: 31).

Holistic concepts that try to keep pace with the development of the whole personality of children should not try to keep up with the development of athletic techniques too soon. The following are some brief holistic ideas for swimming instruction.

1. Teaching Motor Skills

The teaching of motor skills has been defined by a working group studying the psychological motor process as the "concept of developing the personality using motor processes" (Irmischer, 1980: 27). Thus, learning motor techniques for sports is not the most important point of motor pedagogy. It is more the significance of motor activity in the development of the young person's whole personality. Teaching motor skills, as does the psychological motor activity, emphasizes the inseparable connection between movement and perception and the close relationship between movement and the emotional and the cognitive processes (see also Kiphard, 1979; Irmischer, 1980).

2. Ability to React

Many sports instructors believe that the ability to react is the main goal of sports and movement instruction. For swimming instruction, Durlach (1994: 13) notes the following goal: "Teaching children the ability to react when dealing with water".

3. The Concept of Movement as a Dialogue

Hildebrandt sees learning to swim as being "the inclusion of the element water as space in which movement can take place" (1993: 199). He calls for a concept of movement pedagogy for swimming instruction, similar to the one developed by Gordijn. He "sees mobility of the person as being a subjective dialogue between the human being and the world" (Hildebrandt, 1993: 200).

4. The Theory of Teaching Integration

The theory of teaching integration as the education of both handicapped and non-handicapped children, also gives new stimuli for a holistically-oriented education (see also Eberwein, 1994; Kobi, 1994; Zielke, 1994; etc.). Fediuk (1992), Scheid (1995) and Rheker (1995, 1996) have contributed, above all, to the integrative ideas in sports teaching.

The integrative teaching of sport seeks to integrate people with different abilities into the sports lesson and beyond that, and is also based on the holistic approach (cf., Chapter 1.4). The whole human being, with all his strengths and weaknesses, whether handicapped or not, is the center of all teaching efforts. It should be made possible that each human being is permitted to develop his own, individual abilities in society (see also Rheker, 1996b).

These pedagogic theories have the following goals in common: one goal is the **development of the whole personality. Various experiences in movements** are more important than a one-sided learning of techniques. The emphasis is on **enjoying movement, games and sports. Independence during the learning process, inner motivation** and a **life-long, healthy athletic activity** are very important goals, just as is **getting to grips with the environment** (material experience).

In the area of beginners swimming, these teaching theories are very important. In particular, playing and moving in the water offers the beginner ways in which to gain various experiences of movement, to try out their own movements, to be creative, to be part of organizing the teaching and the learning process of beginners swimming together with the instructor, etc. Uncomplicated movement exercises or arranged teaching situations can achieve these goals in all the areas of beginners swimming. Advocates of a more traditional teaching method will be able to get along with the following methodology for beginner swimming. The methodically structured areas permit a sequentially deductive approach, in which the instructor gives the goals and content of the swimming instruction.

Methodical Concepts for Beginner Swimming

The following concept for beginner swimming attempts to put holistic ideas for sports instruction into practice. At the same time it borrows from the proven methods of Lewin and Wilke. It has been tested successfully for more than twenty years in various beginner swimming groups (swimming with babies and infants, swimming with handicapped children and young people, swimming teaching at primary school, swimming teaching at special needs and integrative schools, swimming teaching in sports instructor training).

The following concept was developed: the areas of beginner swimming (underwater diving, breathing, jumping in and diving, floating and gliding) are supplemented by "getting used to the water by having fun" and the "elementary movement experience ", which, following my experience with beginners swimming, are of great importance They are especially important for teaching swimming to very young children, handicapped children and young people. The suggested method for beginners swimming includes the following areas:

1. Getting used to the water by having fun
2. Underwater diving
3. Breathing
4. Diving
5. Floating
6. Gliding
7. Elementary movements

These areas of beginners swimming are introduced in such a way that many different experiences can be gained in each area on different levels. The partial learning goals can be worked on using uncomplicated tasks, while at the same time they can also be learned using precise game and movement instructions.

For example, in the area of *underwater diving*, children can discover that by doing exercises and games in the water, they can leave the ground for a shorter or a longer time by using their feet to exert different amounts of pressure on them. In movement exercises, which require the learner to use creative, varied experimentation, to explore and come up with his own movements, *diving*, in differing ways, can be structured:

- from the steps

- from the edge of the pool

- from the starting block or the diving board

In this method of beginners swimming, the areas "getting used to the water by having fun" and "basic movements" are particularly important. From the very first time in the water up until he can swim safely and going on beyond that, the learner can work at, learn and practice various techniques and movement skills. The process begins by learning to adjust the movements so that an unsure non-swimmer can keep his balance when standing in the water. As he walks through the water the learner experiences the resistance of the water and by using his arms and legs, he can learn the first techniques of forward propulsion.

For people who are already good swimmers, new techniques, such as the somersault turn, can be worked at by doing elementary turning movements in all possible axes (side-ways, head over and diving under). Elements of exhibition and synchronized swimming techniques and "artistic swimming techniques" can promote the swimmer's creativity and choice of movement structure. Thus, the area of "elementary movement" is just not a partial learning goal which is only important for beginners swimming. It is a general goal, which goes from the lessons with beginners up to swimming training, because it contributes to the movement structure and the improvement of coordination while swimming, diving, underwater diving, water polo, synchronized swimming, etc.

Similarly, "getting used to the water by having fun" has a special significance that goes beyond beginners swimming. Using the first games, which, above all, should give the feeling of having fun and movement in water, and were designed to help beginners relax in the water by overcoming their fears and the sense of unfamiliarity with water, swimming instruction for beginners can be made more relaxed. Basic experiences in and under the water can be gained in a playful atmosphere.

After the non-swimmer has become a swimmer, these games can be continued. Besides little ball games ball games in teams or with partners, games such as water polo, water basketball, water volleyball or water football can be introduced. In the same way, little games such as treasure hunting, underwater ball, passing games etc., can be used to practice diving. In addition to these two general areas (see also Figure 27) there are 5 sections that can be designated as techniques for swimming for beginners:

- underwater diving

- breathing

- jumping in and diving

- floating

- gliding

However, these areas cannot be isolated from each other. They all have an affect on each other and overlap. This becomes clear when looking at the following tasks:

- Jumping from the steps or the edge of the pool with the additional task of jumping into a hoop and moving away by diving underwater. The areas of underwater diving and diving overlap.

- Gliding and laying the head on the water (*gliding and underwater diving*).

- Drawing the legs up to the body and breathing out slowly (*floating and breathing*)

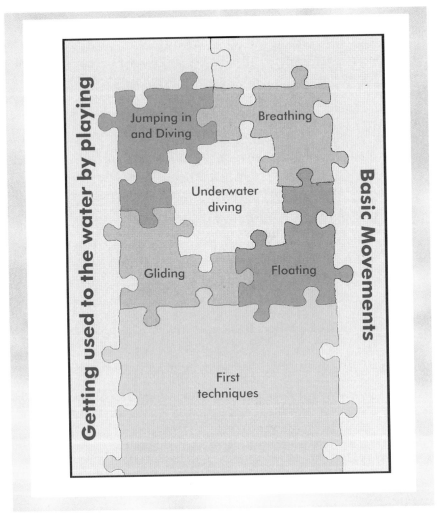

Figure 27: *The Areas of Swimming for Beginners*

Since nearly all of the separate areas overlap others, the common areas cannot be presented clearly in a diagram. The sections are shown as being pieces of a jigsaw puzzle which fit into each other, thus showing the points of contact and overlap.

Jigsaw Puzzle

To make sure that children develop their abilities in sports as fully as possible it is necessary to begin at their level. If you expect too much or too little from children, progress will tend to be slow. If, however, the games and exercises offered are at the level of their abilities and expectations, you will often find they learn more rapidly. At the end of each chapter a check list is given to allow an assessment of the level of ability in that particular learner swimming area. This check list not only allows a quick overview of the level of skill reached, but also gives tips on which system and method structure should be used in order to reach the next stage of development.

2.1   Games for Getting Swimmers Used to the Water

"Playing is experimenting with chance"

(Novalis)

"Games for Getting Swimmers Used to the Water" is a very extensive section, and goes from the beginner swimmer's first time in the water up to the stage of the swimmer inventing his own games. Before introducing the games and their forms, which gives this section a large content, let us have a look at the goals that can be reached by "getting swimmers used to the water by having fun". For this, the goals are divided into four partial learning goals.

2.1.1   The Aims of Getting Used to the Water by Having Fun

1. Emotionally affective learning goals

* Fun and enjoyment:
  Children should have fun and enjoy being in water, playing and moving in it or, by being beside water, or getting into and being under it.
* Reducing fear:
  The intensity of the games should allow anxious children to lose their fear of the water and learn to move in it with more confidence.

- Independence:
  By learning basic abilities like *swimming underwater, gliding and moving forwards* children can free themselves from being dependent on and being the responsibility of adults and thus become independent.
- Self-confidence:
  Self-confidence will grow by managing to do movement exercises which require courage.
- Feelings of success:
  Successfully completing movement exercises will increase the motivation for trying out new things.
- Relaxation and well-being:
  By doing intensive movements and games, tension is reduced. Movement becomes relaxed and free from fear; a physical and psychological state of well-being is achieved by the intentional use of exertion and stimulus.

2. Cognitive Learning Goals

For many beginners, water is an unfamiliar element. Movement in water is subject to other conditions and rules than those prevalent on firm ground.

- Getting to know the water with its various characteristics:
  - viscosity and pressure
  - resistance
  - buoyancy
  - water temperature/the stimulus of coldness
  - wetness (cf., Chapter 1.1)
- Becoming familiar with the swimming pool and swimming rules:
  - getting to know the areas in the facility: the learner's pool, the main swimming pool, the showers, the changing rooms, bathrooms etc
  - swimming and hygiene rules
  - water conditions (temperature, amount of chlorine)
- Getting to know the physical characteristics of the water and using them consciously: e.g., experiencing buoyancy and letting the body float.
- Learning and following game rules.

3. Social Learning Goals

Social learning is important in all groups. Social goals can be achieved through motor activity, especially by using movement, games and sports. In normal school classes often more than 50% of the children demonstrate noticeable motor problems (overweight, coordination problems, etc.,) (cf., Dordel, 1993: 143). Games with socializing aspects are suitable for integrating these children into the class. In many parts of Germany, handicapped children attend normal schools so that they can be taught in integrated classes. This heterogeneity of learning groups should lead to sports and swimming lessons that stress social learning as much as athletic performance. Thus, the following partial learning goals can be defined as:

* playing together
* learning and playing games in which everybody can participate
* using games to improve cooperation
* games for improving communication
* preferring to play games that integrate outsiders and minorities

4. Motor Active Learning Goals

Through the children's confrontation with water, deficits in motor skills can be reduced by using a variety of movements. By beginning with the simple task of keeping one's balance in the water and going on to do specific propulsive movements, certain basic motor skills, and in particular, coordination and stamina can be encouraged.

Swimming instruction plays an important role in achieving the following goals:

* development of the basic characteristics of motor activity; stamina, strength, speed, coordination abilities
* learning a variety of movement patterns
* special movement skills: underwater diving, breathing, diving, floating, gliding, throwing and catching, forward movement in, into and under the water.

2.1.2   The Content of Getting Used to the Water by Having Fun – Games

First we look at some categories of games from a huge range of games for this area. Some games and forms of games in each category are explained in detail with examples. Others will be listed only by name.

Running and Catching Games

→ **Chain catch**

One catcher starts by trying to catch other players. All those caught hold hands with the catcher so that after a while a long chain forms. In this chain only the players at each end of the chain may use their free hand(s) to catch somebody.

Variation: • if the chain has more than 10 people, it can be divided into two or more chains.

→ **Catching and freeing**

Depending on the size of the group, one, two or three catchers try to catch as many people as possible. Those caught make a bridge or stand in the straddle position. They can be freed if players who are not yet caught crawl through their legs.

Variations: • increase the number of catchers
• free the caught players by shaking hands or tapping on the back
• free the caught players by diving through their legs
• vary the way in which they move forward: running, walking, jumping, swimming, paddling etc

→ **Who's afraid of the "white shark"?**

One player, playing the "white shark", stands on the side of the pool, the others stand on the opposite side. The white shark calls out: "Who is afraid of the white shark?" Everybody answers: "Nobody". The white shark calls out: "And if he comes?" Everybody yells out: "Then we all run (dive, swim)". Then everybody runs, dives or swims to the other side. Anyone caught helps the white shark to catch in the next round.

Variation: • White shark in the fog: the catcher is handicapped by 2-4 players, who create "fog" by splashing the water.

→ **"Fisherman, fisherman, how deep is the water?"**

A fisherman, acting as catcher, stands on one side of the pool, with everyone else on the opposite side. Everybody shouts: "Fisherman, fisherman, how deep is the water?" The fisherman answers e.g., "A 1000 fathoms deep". Everybody asks: "How can we get across?" The fisherman specifies the movement to be used, such as, e.g., "by hopping along on one leg" or "running backwards" or any other movement. Anyone caught helps the fisherman to catch in the next round.

Variation: • The way of moving forward can be changed: running, jumping, swimming, diving, paddling, etc.

Additional running and catching games (see also 'Integration through Games and Sports', Rheker, 2000):

- "Fisherman, Fisherman what flag are you showing today?"
- Flying fish
- ABC- Catch
- The Sea calls all Fish
- Copy-cat
- Duck shooting
- Black and white – or Day and Night

- Magic Mouse
- On the spot
- Ox on the hill 1,2,3
- Prison
- Catch the time
- Chain catch in pairs
- Catching animals

These games may be substituted for others with which the instructor and swimmers are more familiar.

2. Ball Games
→ **Wandering ball game**
Two balls are thrown across the circle as quickly as possible, but each time leaving out the direct neighbor. The aim is to catch the other ball up.

Variations: • changing the direction
• catching and throwing with one hand

→ **"Tired, Worn-out, Dead"**
The group forms circles of 6-12 people. Balls are thrown into each circle. Any circle that doesn't catch the ball the first time is "tired", which means that everyone has to kneel. The second time someone doesn't catch the ball, the circle is "worn-out" and everyone has to sit down. If the ball isn't caught the third time, the circle is "dead" and everyone lies down and is out of the game.

Variations: • in the water: tired = up to the shoulders in the water,
worn-out = up to the chin in the water, dead = under
water and out of the game,
  • catching and throwing with one hand
  • calling the first name before throwing
  • clapping the hands before catching the ball

→ **The Ten Pass Game:**
Two teams of same strength, but with different bathing caps, try to keep
the ball for as long as possible by passing and catching it in their own
rows. The team gets a point when it has completed ten passes without
surrendering the ball to the opponent. The opposing team now tries to
pass the ball ten times. If the other team manages to intercept the ball, it
can try immediately to get 10 passes.

Variations: • a point is awarded after 5 or 6 passes
  • you are not allowed to run/ swim with the ball
  • you are not allowed to pass the ball directly back
  • a foul rule is introduced
  • catching and throwing with one hand

→ **Tiger Ball:**
The members of a team stand in a circle and throw the ball to each
other. An opponent in the middle of the circle tries to interrupt them or to
catch the ball. If he is successful in catching or touching the ball, the one
who threw the ball is the new tiger in the middle of the circle.

Variations: • the ball must be passed at a height so that it can be
caught.
  • the number of tigers is increased to 2-4
  • two circles play against each other. The tiger comes from
the opponent's circle and is exchanged by one of his
team, as soon as he has caught the ball. The winner is
the team which is the first to have had all its players as
tigers in the opponent's circle.
  • all players move freely

Additional Ball Games (see also 'Integration through Games and Sports', Rheker, 2000):

- Driving the ball
- Tower Ball
- Passing the ball
- "Volker-Ball"
- Fire Ball
- Ball on the Castle
- Three playing areas
- Water-basketball

- Ball Possession – taboo
- Water Biathlon
- Moving Balls
- Water Volleyball
- Hunter Ball
- Water Football
- Sorting the Balls
- Underwater Ball

3. Relay Games

→ **Running Relay**

Several teams are formed and they stand at one side of the learner's pool. The players now run to a turning point (e.g. the edge of the pool on the other side) in a relay. The winning team is the one all the members of which have run the distance.

Variations: • run forwards, backwards or sideways
• hopping, jumping, or moving forwards in other ways
• doing frog-jumps through the water

→ **Pushing Relay**

The players form several teams which stand at one side of the pool. The first player in each team pushes the second team member to the other side of the pool. He then runs back and pushes the third across, and so on, until all players are at the other side of the pool.

→ **Clothes Relay**

In this relay the first player of each team puts on a T-shirt, a bathing cap and flippers. He then swims to the turning point and back. He gives the "clothes" to the next member in the team. The winning team is the one which is the first to have all its members run the distance "clothed".

Variations: • life saving clothes must be worn (jacket, trousers) and flippers
• funny, or clothes reflecting the season can be worn, e.g., Santa Claus costumes, carnival costumes, etc.

→ **Hanger-on Relay**
The runners of a team are supposed to complete a distance as quickly as possible, as in all relays. In the hanger-on relay the first player runs around a marked point and fetches the second player. Both run again and fetch the third player and so on.

Variations: • when all players are "attached" they are "uncoupled" by running in the opposite order
• in the water: run or swim

Additional Relay Games (see also 'Integration through Games and Sports', Rheker, 2000):

- Relief Relay
- Water Biathlon
- Pull Relay
- Underwater Ball (carrying)
- Carrying Relay
- Underwater Ball – Marathon Relay

- Diving Relay
- Treasure Hunt Relay
- Obstacle Relay
- Chain Relay
- Creative Relay
  Dribbling the ball on the water

4. Games in a Circle and Singing Games
→ "Eenie, Miny, Mo"

Photo 5: *The game " Eenie, Miny, Mo "*

All players hold hands and form a circle. One player is the catcher and stands in the middle. Everyone sings and jumps:

"Eenie, , Miny, mo,
A fish has bit my toe,
Eeny miny mick
Swim away quick"

After the last word everyone tries to get to or swim to the edge of the pool as quickly as possible, while the catcher tries to catch at least one person before he reaches the edge of the pool. If the catcher is successful, the person caught is the new catcher in the center of the circle.

Variations: • singing loudly and jumping
• singing quietly and making as small a jump as possible
• all catchers remain catchers so that the number of catchers increases steadily

→ "Show your feet"
Everyone stands in a circle and sings the songs below. The player's do actions to represent the songs which help those learning to get used to the water.
Chorus:

"Show me your feet   *(everyone lifts the right foot in the air)*
show me your shoes   *(everyone lifts the left foot in the air)*
and let's see what we can do:
(1) I'm going to wash that man
right out of my hair.....   *(everyone washes the hair, face and other parts of the body)*

Chorus: Show me your feet etc...
(2) Dashing away with the
smoothing iron...   *(everyone pretends to iron close to the surface of the water and by doing so, sprays each other)*

Chorus: Show..etc...
(3) I'm for ever blowing bubbles ...   *(everyone blows air into the water to make bubbles)*

Chorus: Show...
(4) I could have danced all night...   *(everyone dances around in two's or three's holding on to each other and kicking up spray over the others)*

Chorus: Show...

Additional Circle and Singing Games: (see also 'Integration through Games and Sports', Rheker, 2000):

- Here we go round the mulberry bush
- I sent a letter to my love
- Bingo
- Ring-a-ring o' roses
- Two Fat Gentlemen
- Dancing in circles

- Heads and shoulders
- Up I stretch
- Knees and toes
- Looby loo
- Aram sam sam
- You twiddle your fingers and clap your hands

5. Communication Games
→ **Molecular game**
All players move to the rhythm of music in the learner's pool. When the music stops, the leader of the game indicates, either visually or acoustically, which people should get together to form a group. The groups now get different tasks, which can focus on different themes.

→ **Communication, Getting to know one another**
- asking the names of the others in the group
- talking with each other
- interviewing the others on special topics

→ **Movement tasks:**
- move about the room as a group
- which group can make itself the smallest/biggest?
- which group builds the most creative tower (not the highest)?

→ **Name Ball:**
All players stand in a circle and throw the ball to each other. The one who throws must say the name of the catcher before throwing.

Variation:
- before catching the catcher must clap hands twice
- catching and throwing with one hand

→ **Copy-cat:**
Everybody looks for a partner. One partner moves through the learner's pool doing as many different movements as possible. The other follows

him like a shadow and copies his partner. After two or three minutes they change places.

Variations: • different paths through the pool
• varying the paths, the speed and movements
• the shadow makes different movements to his partner in the water

Additional Games: (see also 'Integration through Games and Sports', Rheker, 2000):

• The welcome game
• Mirror
• Shake hands
• Dance of the Magnets
• Dancing down the path
• Leading the blind

6. Interactive Games

→ **Partner, Help**
A catcher tries to catch the others. When he has almost caught somebody this player is allowed to call: "Partner, help!" If some one manages to take his hand, neither player can be caught. Any player caught is the new catcher.

Variations: • two or more catchers, depending on the size of the group
• anyone caught becomes a catcher
• variations of the movements

→ **Ball possession – Taboo**
A catcher tries to catch the other team-members. When he has almost caught somebody, someone else throws this player a ball. The catcher now has to find somebody else to catch. Any player caught is the new catcher.

Variations: • two or more catchers
• two or more balls
• anyone caught becomes a catcher

→ **ABC-Catch**

All players move in groups of three through the pool. The three players run or walk close to each other in a group. Each of the three gets a name: A, B or C. When the leader of the game calls "A" for Alpha, A runs off, while B and C have to hold hands and catch A. Then all three walk together side by side again, until e.g. "C" for Charlie is called and A and B are the catchers.

Variations:
- players run or hop
- walking backwards, walking sideways
- those not called, hook in with their arms for the catch
- the catchers swim next to each other and try to catch the third

→ **Virus Game**

The virus game is a catching game. Anyone caught is infected and lies down in the water or floats. He can be freed when two "healthy" people take hold of his hands and feet and bring him to the hospital (e.g. the steps in the learner's pool). While being brought to the hospital nobody can be caught. The catcher represents the virus.

Additional games: (see also 'Integration through Games and Sports', Rheker, 2000):

- Catching and Freeing
- Dressing up games
- Molecular Game
- Hanger-On Relay
- Shake Hands

- Crossing the bridge
- Magic Mouse
- Never-ending Hunter Ball
- Copy-cat
- Making waves

7. Acting Games

→ **Moving Through the Water like Animals**

All the children move through the water like animals. They can use their fantasy and pretend to be different animals.

Variations:
- hopping like frogs
- galloping like horses
- trampling like elephants
- walking like a stork, etc

→ **The Sea calls all the Fishes**

Every child chooses what kind of fish he wants to be. For example, the dolphins are then sent to one corner of the learner's pool, the sharks to another, the goldfish into the third corner and the other flatfish into the fourth corner. The leader of the game stays in the middle of the pool and represents the sea. The sea calls the fish to come. The fish then come into the middle of the learner's pool as the 'sea'. They copy everything the sea does, e.g., when the sea is very calm, all the fish become quiet and lie quietly on the water. Then the sea starts making little waves. A wind blows and the waves get bigger. There can also be a hurricane or a spring tide. When the sea suddenly calls "high tide" all fish must get back to their corners quickly, otherwise they are caught. Caught fish now help the sea at catching.

→ **Duck hunt**

A hunter tries to catch the others (the "ducks"). When the hunter comes the ducks can dive, i.e., if the head is held under the water the player cannot be caught.

Variations: • the hunter throws a soft water ball to hit the others
• the number of hunters increases

Additional acting games:
• Fisherman, fisherman how deep is the water?
• Animal movements to music
• Acting from daily life
• Molecular game
• Show your feet
• The Wild West
• This little pig went to market
• Hopping like a frog

8. Strength and Ability Games

→ **Pulling Fights**

Two partners stand opposite each other, holding each other by the right hand and trying to pull the opponent onto the other side.

→ **Push the Partner away**

Two partners stand opposite each other, 1 meter apart. Each puts his hands on the other's shoulders and tries to make his opponent lose balance.

→ **Group Pulling Fight**
Two groups stand opposite each other with gaps between them. Everyone uses the right hand to hold the right hand of the player to his right and his left hand to hold the left hand of the player to his left (a zigzag arrangement). Which group can succeed in pulling the other over the line drawn on the ground?

Variation: • pushing fight: instead of pulling, they push

→ **Hen and Fox/ Pike and Carp**
The members of one team stand behind each other with their hands on the hips of the person in front. The first member of the group stands in front as the fox. The second member then becomes a hen that wants to protect the others, the chicks, behind him by opening his wings (arms). The fox tries to catch the last chick. If he is successful, the fox becomes a hen and the chick that has been caught becomes the fox.

Variation: • the size of the group can vary

Additional strength and ability games:

- Escape from being caught
- Obstacle course
- Running a Slalom
- Dressing up Games

- Diving in a Slalom
- Carrying Relay
- Water Biathlon
- Carriage and Pair

9. Games for Experiencing the Body
→ Floating lying on the front or the back (see Chapter 2.5.)

→ Relaxation exercises and games

10. Games for techniques of getting used to the water
→ Games for underwater diving

→ Games for breathing

→ Games for diving

→ Games for floating

→ Games for gliding

2.2 Underwater Diving

"Let the water flow that you cannot drink."

(Columbian Proverb)

2.2.1 The Basics of Underwater Diving

The term 'underwater diving' means intentionally getting under the surface of the water, being able to orient oneself and move about underwater.

The following reflexes are very important in underwater diving:

- **The eye protective reflex action**
  Usually the eyelids protect our eyes from harmful external influences by closing on reflex. They do this automatically, i.e., as a reflex action, when foreign objects come too close to the eyes. Thus, our eyes are protected, when a twig moves quickly in our direction during a walk through the forest. When diving with the head underwater, the eye protects itself using the same mechanism. This reflex can be overcome by deliberately opening the eyes underwater.

- **The head reflexive action**
  The head reflexive action tries to protect the body from injury by lifting the head up when falling forwards. This reflexive action is a hindrance when wanting to practice the best position in the water during gliding or a dive headfirst, because it makes the head move towards the back of the neck. The reflexive action has to be overcome by using specific exercises and games. The reflexive action can be overcome by using exercises such as rolling into the water or jumping from the steps through a hoop.

- **The breathing reflex**
  Breathing ensures that we do not hold our breath for too long. Many people are afraid of suffocating underwater, because they cannot get any air. Diving suppresses the breathing reflex and allows a conscious regulation of breathing.

2.2.2 Teaching *Underwater Diving* in Beginners Swimming

The following introduces a methodical concept in teaching beginners underwater diving. The suggestions for games and exercises presented here should be regarded as one source of ideas. They can be supplemented by many other games and exercises thought up by the instructor or his pupils.

The ability to dive underwater can also be worked on holistically, but the systematic build-up of exercises in the series of exercises underwater diving (see Figure 28) should be seen as a guide.

If games and exercises are turned into a gripping story, as is possible in project instruction, they soon lose the character of being just exercises and thus provide good motivation for the children. Such ideas for games can be included in topics like pirate ships, treasure hunts, submarines, underwater caves etc. Here is one story as an example:

A pirate ship is built using floats and swimming bars, and is put to sea carrying a heavy freight of treasure (stones wrapped in aluminum foil, rubber rings, cutlery e.g. spoons, old coffee pots and children's toys). The pirate ship now moves further out to sea and is caught up in a storm. It swings and sways wildly from side to side. The waves enter the boat, and it loses a part of its cargo. The storm worsens so much that the ship capsizes and all the treasure sinks into the sea (learners' pool). When the storm is over, the brave pirates try to recover the treasure from the bottom of the sea by sending the first divers off to retrieve the treasure. Diving teams can be formed to try and retrieve as much treasure as possible.

Figure 28: *Underwater Diving*

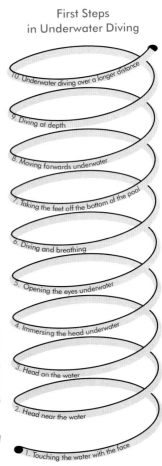

First Steps
in Underwater Diving

10. Underwater diving over a longer distance

9. Diving at depth

8. Moving forwards underwater

7. Taking the feet off the bottom of the pool

6. Diving and breathing

5. Opening the eyes underwater

4. Immersing the head underwater

3. Head on the water

2. Head near the water

1. Touching the water with the face

The Methodical Way to Dive

The section on *underwater diving* is divided into various partial learning goals:

A prerequisite for putting the head under water is the ability to "close the mouth". Only those who can close their mouths at will are able to keep their mouth closed under water so that it cannot enter during diving. For this reason, for anyone who has difficulty in closing his mouth, such as people with spastic handicaps, exercises should be given on closing the mouth at the beginning of the swimming instruction. The following exercises are suitable for this:

- blowing exercises (also see the section on *Breathing*, Chapter 2.3)
- holding one's breath when still on dry land, under the shower, and in the water
- closing the mouth when water is splashed
  (For additional games see also the 2nd partial learning goal: placing the head closer to the surface of the water)

As nervous children are afraid of resting the head on the water, similar exercises and games should be carried out at the beginning of these exercises for underwater swimming.

1. Partial Learning Goal: Touching the water with the face

The following exercises and games are designed to get children[3] to lose their fear of having water splashed on their faces. The children's degree of involvement in the games distracts them from any fears they may have. They can get used to water spraying in the face when playing and associate this as being normal; turning this aspect positively into having fun whilst playing in the water.

Games and Exercises
→ Taking a shower
  The children take a shower together and learn that water can run over all parts of the body and over the head.

  Variations: • varying the temperature of the water
  • taking a shower and splashing the water
  • alternating hot and cold showers

[3]The goals for swimming for beginners are presented for "children" as a target group, but this can also include older children, young and older people.

→ **Splashing water with the feet**:
The children are sitting, spread out along the edge of the pool with their legs dangling in the water. When a signal is given, they splash the water with their legs.

Variations:
- using only one leg
- moving the legs at different speeds
- splashing water with the hands and feet
- drumming the legs whilst lying on their stomachs
- making the water "boil" with their legs

→ **Splashing the others until they are soaked**
One part of the group stands in the water at the steps in front of the rest of the group. Those sitting on the steps are now allowed to splash the others until they are soaked.

Variations: see above

→ **Washing games**
A hoop is placed on the water. This hoop represents a washbowl or washtub. The children stand around this "tub" and start to wash themselves. First the hands and arms are washed, then the face and so on.

Variations:
- washing one's partner
- washing oneself or the partner with a sponge or a flannel

→ **Watering flowers**
All children can choose what kind of flower they want to be. One child is chosen to be the gardener, who is allowed to water the flowers.

Variations:
- watering with cupped hands
- watering with a water can

→ **Circle and singing games**, in which water is splashed "by accident"
- "Eenie, miny, mo"
- "I'm going to wash that man right out of my hair"
- Ring o' ring of Roses
- "Show us your feet"

→ **Running and catching games**, in which water is splashed onto faces "by accident"
- "Who is afraid of the White Shark?" (especially the variation with fog)
- "The sea calls all the fish"
- Duck hunting
- "Fisherman, fisherman how deep is the water?"
  (For additional games, see also 'Integration through Games and Sports, Rheker, 2000)

2. Partial Learning Goal: **Head near the water**

The aim of the following games and exercises is to bring the head closer and closer to the surface of the water. This will overcome those attempts by nervous children to keep the head as far away as possible from the unknown element of water.

Games and Exercises
→ **Regatta sailing**
The children blow corks, soap dishes or little ships over the water. Anyone wanting to accomplish this has to move his mouth closer to the surface of the water.

Variations:
- competition sailing: All "boats" start on one side of the learner's pool and are blown to the other side as quickly as possible.
- sailing relay: the children form teams and they sail in competitive relays.
- regatta during a storm: some of the children stir the water up, make sailing difficult: soft waves, big waves, hurricane etc.

→ **Competition Blowing**
Two children have a cork (little ship) and one tries to blow the cork towards the partner.

Variations:
- a number of children stand around a small lake (hoop) and try to blow the ship (or several ships) on the lake to the other side
- the children use a straw to blow the corks around in the water

→ **Pushing balls over the water**
Each child tries to move a ball from one side of the pool to the other, using the head.

Variations: • pushing balls in a relay
  • various balls are pushed forwards with the head: lightweight balls, balloons, ordinary balls etc.
  • the children move the balls around in the water using different parts of the body: hands, elbow, mouth, nose, forehead, knee.

Additional games
• blowing a hole in the water   • relay races
• fire brigade pump   • "Show us your feet"

3. Partial Learning Goal: Head on the water

Children should learn first to rest parts of their heads (e.g. the mouth, the left ear, the nose) and then the whole head on the water.

Games and Exercises:
→ **Washtub**
rules – see above

Variation: • the face is pushed into the washtub

→ **Glass-bottom Boat**
A hoop is placed on the water to represent the glass bottom through which the children can watch the fish in the sea by resting their head on the water

→ **Diving along the edge of the pool**
The children hold on to the edge of the pool and with their faces under water, they move sideways, holding on to the overflow gutter.

Variations: • the children are guided through the water by others holding their hands, while the person being guided rests his face on the water
  • the children move freely without a "guide" with their heads in the water and examine the bottom of the sea (searching for treasure etc.)

4. Partial Learning Goal: Immersing the head underwater

The children learn to immerse their heads completely.

Games and Exercises:
→ **Immersing parts of the head:**
The children keep hold of the edge of the pool and immerse their heads as far as their chins (mouth, nose, forehead, ears).

→ **Immersing the whole head:**
One partner hold hands with the other. Taking it in turns, they go into a squatting position in the water and in doing so, completely immerse the head.

Variation: • everyone stands in a circle and holds hands. Every second person goes into a deep squatting position, immersing the head as far as he wants to

→ **Diving underneath things:**
Two children hold a hoop. The third dives from underneath up through the hoop and back again.

Variations: • going under a swimming board (swimming bar, swimming lane line, etc.)
• going through hoops that are held vertically

→ **Using the head to toss objects into the air:**
Diving under a swimming board (pull-buoy, swimming bar etc.) and using the head to toss the object into the air.

→ **Singing a song under water:**
One child sings a simple song under water. The others rest their heads on or put their heads under the water and try to guess what song it is.

Additional games:
• fire brigade pump
• "This little piggy went to market"
• "I'm going to wash that man right out of my hair" and others

Aquafun – First Steps

5. Partial Learning Goal: Opening the eyes underwater

The children learn to open the eyes under water and to orientate themselves.

Games and Exercises:

→ Putting the face onto the water and opening the eyes:
The children put their faces onto the water and open the eyes in order to get their bearings.

> Variations: • going into the squatting position, putting the head under water and opening the eyes for orientation.

→ Retrieving objects out of the water:
Various things (rubber rings, diving stones, treasure etc.) are spread about on the bottom of the learner's pool. The children have to retrieve them.

> Variations: • retrieving objects (rubber rings, treasure etc.) from different heights at the steps.
> • retrieving objects out of hip-deep water
> • retrieving objects out of chest-deep water
> • retrieving objects out of shoulder-deep water

→ Pulling faces:
Diving with a partner, looking at each other and pulling faces.

→ Counting fingers:
One partner shows a specific number of fingers underwater. The other partner has to see and name them.

→ Moving things under water:
Various objects are held and moved underwater.
• pressing a ball under the water and watching it come up
• the partner moves objects (bathing caps, rubber rings, etc.) about under the water, the other has to follow the objects with his eyes and catch hold of them.

→ **Flotsam and Jetsam:**
Various objects (rubber rings, diving stones, treasures etc.) are spread about on the bottom of the learner's pool. The pupils stand at the steps. When a start signal is given the children try to retrieve as many objects as possible out of the water.

Variations: • each child is only allowed to bring one treasure back to the steps each time he dives
   • Flotsam and Jetsam Relay: One player from each team goes off to retrieve one piece of treasure. As soon as this treasure is brought back to the team, the next member of the team goes off, and so on.

→ **Making figures under water:**
Various objects are spread about under water so that they form figures. The children have to dive from one object to another to try to identify the figures.

6. Partial Learning Goal: Diving and breathing

The children learn to breathe out under water and overcome its resistance. Some of the exercises used here are the same as those in the section on Breathing, so not all will be explained in detail.

Games and Exercises:
→ Blowing a hole in the water
→ Blowing a table tennis ball over the water
→ Breathing out and going slowly into the squatting position
→ **Sea lion:** bellowing into the water like a sea lion
→ **Fire brigade pump:**
Two partners hold hands. One partner squats down underneath the water and breathes out. When he surfaces again, the other partner goes down and breathes out.
→ **Sinking:**
The children breathe out slowly, letting themselves sink onto the bottom of the pool.
→ **Diving against the clock:**
The children dive and try to hold their breath for a length of time.

Variations: • diving against time with a partner: One partner dives while the other counts how long he stays under the water
• Who can stay underwater the longest?

7. Partial Learning Goal: **Taking the feet off the bottom of the pool**

The children learn to take their feet off the bottom of the pool when diving.

Games and Exercises:

Games with the help of a partner

→ **Hopping in a circle:**
All the children stand in a circle holding hands. They hop up into the air and every second child then dives underwater.

→ **Hopping and diving while standing in a circle, playing games and/or singing:**
- Eenie, miny, mo

→ **Elevator:**
Two children stand in front of each other. One child stands with his legs closed. The other pulls himself towards the bottom of the pool by holding onto the legs of his partner.

→ **Who can sit on the bottom of the pool?**
All the children try to sit on the bottom of the learner's pool. Everybody finds a suitable place.

→ **Pull and dive:**
Using a rod or hoop, two partners pull a third with his head underwater through the water.

→ **Diving like a Dolphin:**
Two children hold a rod, a piece of rope or a hoop. A third child dives through the hoop (or over the rod or the rope) into the water with a dolphin jump.

→ **Merry-go-round:**
All the children stand in a circle holding hands. Every second child lies down on the water while the others make sure that he is being held securely. The people standing begin to move in a circle.

Variations: • every second child lies on his stomach
• every second child lies on his back
• the children are allowed to paddle with the legs
• the circle moves to the right
• the circle moves to the left
• the merry-go-round changes direction very quickly
• the circle moves inwards towards the middle and back again

Games and exercises for teaching the children to keep their legs off the bottom of the pool

→ **Moving hand over hand on the steps:**
The children are in a "press-up" position (the hands are on the pool steps or on the floor). They move themselves forwards using their hands. While they do this they breathe in deeply, simultaneously lifting their heads up and then breathing out again into the water.

→ **Moving hand-over-hand on a rope,** on the rope between the lanes or the overflow gutter: The children move hand over hand along a rope or along the overflow gutter.

→ **Searching for treasure** in chest-deep water (see above).

→ **Diving like a Dolphin:**
See above

Variations: • doing a dolphin jump through a hoop
• doing several dolphin jumps one after another

→ **Cat and Mouse:**
The pupils form a circle, facing each other. A few children are in the middle of the circle representing mice. Outside the circle is a pupil playing the cat who tries to stalk and catch the mice.

Variations: • the "cat" is allowed to come into the circle as well
• the people forming the circle help the mice
• when caught, the mouse becomes a 'cat'

→ **Over and under:**
A team consists of several pairs of pupils holding hands, arranged in a long row. When the start signal is given, the first pair climbs over the arms of the first couple and dive underneath the arms of the next.

8. Partial Learning Goal: Moving forward underwater

The children learn to move under water first with the help of a partner and later on, on their own.

Games and exercises

→ **Diving through their partner's straddled legs:**
One partner stands with straddled legs so that the other can dive through them.
N.B.: Always dive through from the front of the partner so that he can see how deep you have dived and, if need be, help you to get through.

→ **Diving in turns:**
Two children take turns to throw a rubber ring. The child doing the retrieving isn't allowed to do so until the ring reaches the bottom of the pool.

→ **Diving a figure eight:**
One swimmer swims in a figure eight through the straddled legs of the partner.

→ **Eel:**
One child wriggles along underwater around the other members of his group, who are standing in the pool.

→ **Diving through a hoop:**
One partner holds a hoop under water, the other dives through it.

   Variations: • diving through two hoops
            • diving through two hoops held in different positions
            • diving through several hoops

→ **Tunnel-Diving:**
Several partners stand one behind another with straddled legs. One child now can dive through this tunnel.

   Variation: • tunnel-diving as a relay

→ Walking through an underwater cave: see below

→ Walking on the hands:

    Variations: • who can walk or stand on his hands in the learner's pool?
                • who can walk on his hands over the longest distance?

Photo 6: *Walking on the hands through the pool*

9. Partial Learning Goal: Diving at depth

The children learn to dive to a specific location.

Games and Exercises:

→ Retrieving objects from different depths of water:

    Variations: • retrieving objects from the 3rd step to the 1st step
                • retrieving objects out of hip-deep water
                • retrieving objects out of chest-deep water
                • retrieving objects out of neck-deep water
                • retrieving objects from a depth of 2 m

→ **Handstand in the chest-deep water** (see above)

→ **Searching for treasure** in water that is getting deeper

→ **Diving, breathing out.** Letting oneself sink to the bottom of the pool

→ **Diving feet-first**

→ **Diving headfirst**

10. Partial Learning Goal: **Underwater diving over a longer distance**

The children learn techniques that they can use to move forwards underwater.

Games and Exercises:

→ **Who can dive the furthest?**
All pupils start from the edge of the pool or from the steps. They place their feet at the wall/steps and when the signal is given they push themselves off.

→ **Tunnel diving** – see above

→ **Walking through an underwater cave:** Two or three children hold hoops one behind the other in the water. The rest try to dive through this cave.

> *Variations:* • five hoops are held underwater
> • the "cave" has curves
> • at the end of the cave is a treasure which has to be retrieved

→ **Slalom diving:** Several partners stand next to each other in a row so that their straddled legs form a slalom course. Each child dives through this course once.

> *Variations:* • slalom diving as a relay
> • slalom diving around underwater slalom poles
> • diving through the straddled legs of a couple of partners
> • diving through a number of hoops being held up or through hoops on the ground.

→ **Long distance underwater diving:** Who can dive the longest distance?

> *Variations:* • diving across the width of the learner's pool
> • diving across the width of the main pool
> • diving down the full length of the pool as far as possible

→ **Jumping and Diving:**
Jumping into the water and diving:

> *Variations:* • jumping from the steps into the water and diving
> • jumping from the edge of the pool into the water and diving

11. Partial Learning Goal: **The ABC of diving**

a) Games to accustom the children 'A' to flippers
b) Games to accustom the children 'B' to goggles
c) Games to accustom the children 'C' to the snorkel
d) Games and exercises using all the above equipment

*The following checklist gives a brief overview of a pupil's underwater **diving** abilities. At the same time it also gives tips on further measures to achieve this learning goal.*

Checklist: Diving

Partial Learning Goals	Level of Ability		Comments	Game/ Exercise
	yes	no		
1. Touching the water with the face				
• fear of getting water on the face				
• cautiously washing the face				
• water on the face while showering				
• letting water splash onto the face, and wiping it away				
• letting water splash onto the face, without wiping it away				
2. Head near the water				
• standing and moving in hip-deep water				
• standing and moving in chest-deep water				
• immersion up to the shoulders				
• immersion up to the chin				
3. Head on the water				
• up to the mouth				
• up to the nose				
• one ear on the water				
• resting the face briefly on the water				
• resting the whole face in the water				

Partial Learning Goals	Level of Ability		Comments	Game/ Exercise
	yes	no		
4. Immersing the head underwater				
• face on the water				
• face briefly underwater				
• whole head underwater				
• keeping head longer underwater (x seconds)				
• head underwater and blowing bubbles				
5. Opening the eyes underwater				
• resting head on the water and opening the eyes				
• immersing head and opening eyes				
• head into the water, opening the eyes, seeing objects or retrieving them from the stairs				
6. Diving and breathing				
• consciously breathing on the surface of the water				
• resting the face on the surface of the water, exhaling into the water				
• immersing head and exhaling				
• exhaling slowly under water				
• rhythmical breathing (breathing in quickly, breathing out slowly)				
7. Taking the feet off the bottom of the pool				
• with the help of a partner at the steps				
• without the help of partner at the stairs				
• climbing down the legs of a partner				
• retrieving objects out of hip-deep water				
• retrieving objects out of chest-deep water				
8. Moving forward underwater				
• diving under a partner's hand				
• diving through the partner's legs				
• diving through a hoop held under water				
• diving through a number of hoops				
• tunnel diving				
• slalom diving				

Partial Learning Goals	Level of Ability yes no		Comments	Game/ Exercise
9. Diving at depth				
• retrieving objects out of the water at the steps				
3rd step				
2nd step				
1st step				
• retrieving objects out of hip-deep water				
• retrieving objects out of chest-deep water				
• retrieving objects out of neck-deep water				
• retrieving objects from a depth of 2 m				
10. Diving underwater over a longer distance				
• diving through a partner's legs				
• diving through a number of hoops				
• tunnel diving				
• slalom diving				
• X meter diving				
11. The ABC of diving				
• diving with 'A' flippers				
• diving with 'B' goggles				
• diving with 'C' goggles and flippers				
• diving with all the equipment				

2.3   Breathing

2.3.1   The Basics of Breathing

The term **breathing** means the processes essential for life by which our body is supplied with oxygen. A distinction is made between *external* and *internal* breathing. *External* breathing means that oxygen in the air in the lungs is supplied to the blood and carbon dioxide is expelled. *Internal* breathing supplies the tissue (muscles, brain etc.) with oxygen. At the same time carbon dioxide passes into the blood.

Correct, deliberate and rhythmical breathing is very important for swimming. For children, breathing while swimming is done under difficult conditions. Regular and full breathing in and out is very important while swimming in order to maintain the rhythmic movements of the various swimming styles. Children first have to learn how to do this deliberate breathing.

The following difficulties must be taken into account when introducing the breathing exercises:

- Even breathing in chest-deep water can be difficult for children. The pressure of the water on the chest and abdomen makes breathing in more difficult. This pressure can lead to cramping and feelings of fear, especially in children with little experience of swimming, small children or people with specific handicaps (asthma, spastic paralysis etc.)

- Breathing out can also be difficult for children. When breathing out into the water the children have to overcome pressure against the mouth and nose and have to learn not to breathe out suddenly but gently and steadily. Beginners are not used to the higher water resistance when exhaling air from their lungs. They are also not used to air bubbles surfacing in their faces. Getting used to such things can be speeded up with the help of suitable exercises at home (e.g., in the bath).

In order not to cause too much stress for the anxious beginner swimmer (child or adult), the first steps to learning breathing should be structured very simply. Beginning with simple breathing exercises outside the pool, rhythmical breathing is introduced gradually in small steps by breathing in chest-deep water, in the same way swimming techniques are taught later on.

2.3.2 Systematic Breathing Methods

Breathing is divided into the following partial learning goals:

1. Partial Learning Goal: **Keeping the mouth closed/holding the breath**

Children have to learn to close the mouth voluntarily and to hold their breath.

Games and Exercises

→ Holding the breath when not in the water:
Conscious breathing in and holding the breath for a short length of time

Variations: • Breathing in deeply and holding the breath
• Who can hold their breath the longest?

→ **Exhaling exercises** on dry land and in the water (see PLG 2-4)

→ Resting the face on the water and holding the breath

→ Immersing the head and holding the breath

→ With a partner, taking it in turns diving underwater

→ Standing in a circle and holding the breath: Who can stay underwater the longest?

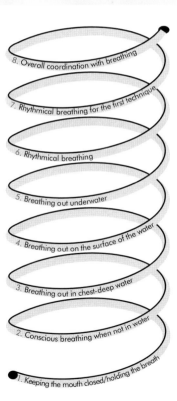

8. Overall coordination with breathing

7. Rhythmical breathing for the first technique

6. Rhythmical breathing

5. Breathing out underwater

4. Breathing out on the surface of the water

3. Breathing out in chest-deep water

2. Conscious breathing when not in water

1. Keeping the mouth closed/holding the breath

2. Partial Learning Goal: **Conscious breathing when not in water**
The children learn to breath in and out deliberately.

Games and Exercises
→ **Conscious breathing in and out on dry land:**
Standing out of the pool everyone breathes in and out together long and deeply. The breathing process, normally done automatically, becomes a conscious act.

Variations: • deliberate breathing in and out with the support of the arms
• breathing in deeply and holding the breath, then breathing out
• who can hold their breath the longest?

3. Partial Learning Goal: **Breathing out in chest-deep water**
The children learn to breathe in and out consciously in chest-deep water.

Games and Exercises
→ Conscious breathing in and out as the pupil moves into deeper water

→ Conscious breathing in and out with the support of the arms

4. Partial Learning Goal: **Breathing out on the surface of the water**
The children learn to deliberately breathe out on the surface of the water.

Games and Exercises
→ **Blowing a hole in the water:**
Who can blow strongly enough to make hole?

→ **Blowing table tennis balls, ships over the water**

→ **Blowing competition:**
Two children have a cork (little ship) between them and the one tries to blow this cork to the other

Variation: • a number of children stand around a little lake (hoop) and try to blow the ship (or ships) to the other side of the lake

→ **Regatta sailing, blowing relays:** see section on underwater diving

→ Blowing bubbles:
Blowing the air out through the mouth on the surface of the water to create bubbles.

Variations: • who can make the loudest bubbles?
• who can blow bubbles the longest?
• who can bubble a recognizable tune?
• who can breathe out through their nose?
• who can breathe out through their mouth and nose?

5. Partial Learning Goal: **Breathing out under water**

Games and Exercises
The children learn to breathe out underwater.
→ Go into the squatting position with the help of a partner and breathe out

→ Keep hold of the edge of the pool and breathe out underwater:

Variations: • breathing out under water through the mouth
• breathing out through the nose
• breathing out through mouth and nose

→ Blowing bubbles into the water

Photo 7: *Blowing bubbles in a group is fun*

→ **Sea lion:** Who can bellow into the water like a sea lion?

→ **Moving forwards** through shallow water by using the arms on the floor of the pool and repeatedly breathing out into the water

→ **Giant and dwarf:**
Breathing out into the water while crouching down small, and then breathing in while stretching up

Additional games:
* Underwater diving one after another
* Fire brigade pump
* "Show us your feet"

6. Partial Learning Goal: **Rhythmical breathing**

This partial learning goal allows a progression from an unconscious breathing rhythm to the breathing rhythm required while doing swimming techniques (strokes): breathing out slowly into the water and breathing in quickly.

Games and Exercises
→ **Rhythmical breathing:**
The children try to breathe out into the water for as long as possible and then breathe in quickly.

Variations:
* breathing out slowly and breathing in quickly on the surface of the water.
* keeping hold of the edge of the pool and breathing out slowly into the water, then lifting the head to breathe in quickly
* in a press-up position at the steps: breathing out slowly into the water and breathing in quickly
* walking through the water with the head resting on the water: breathing out slowly into the water and breathing in quickly
* one partner pulls the other by his stretched arms: the partner who is being pulled breathes out slowly into the water and breathes in quickly

In all exercises the aim to work up to is to have the swimmers breathe out through mouth and nose, and breathe in through the mouth only. Breathing out through the mouth and the nose expels water that has got into the nose. During the breathing exercises, breathing out should last twice as long as breathing in. For the coordination of the swimming techniques it is important to fit the breathing rhythm correctly to the rhythmical actions of each of the swimming strokes.

8. Partial Learning Goal: **Rhythmical breathing to suit the first technique**

The children learn to deliberately breathe in and out in a manner appropriate to the first swimming technique (stroke).

Whereas, during the previous games and exercises, the manner in which one breathed in was unimportant, it is now necessary for the head to be moved to accommodate the breathing rhythm appropriate to the swimming technique. In the crawl stroke, the head is turned to one side; in the breaststroke it is lifted.

Games and Exercises
→ Rhythmical breathing for the crawl:
The rhythmical breathing is carried out in the gliding phase that is required in the crawl. The head stays in the water and is turned to one side to breathe in.

Variations: • in a press-up position at the stairs breathing out slowly into the water, and then turning the head to one side to quickly breathe in
• as above, only turning the head to the other side to breathe in
• with one arm holding the overflow gutter the learner stands at the edge of the pool with the upper part of the body leaning forwards: the learner breathes out slowly into the water and then turns the head quickly to one side to breathe in
• one partner pulls the other through the water by his outstretched arms. The partner who is being pulled now breathes in quickly to one side and then breathes out slowly into the water

- as above, but with leg movement
- rhythmical breathing but now adding the arm stroke (see methodical way for the total coordination of the crawl, Chapter 3.5)

→ **Rhythmical breathing for the breaststroke:**
Breathing in the breaststroke is carried out rhythmically and coordinated. When breathing in, the head is lifted, when breathing out it is lowered back onto the water again.

Variations: • breathing out slowly in a press-up position at the steps while in the water; lifting the head quickly when breathing in
• for other variations, see above

9. Partial Learning Goal: Overall coordination with breathing

The children learn to incorporate rhythmical breathing with the first swimming technique.

Breathing rhythmically is first carried out in a standing position, doing a one-sided arm movement of the crawl stroke. Then both sides of the crawl stroke are practiced. Rhythmical breathing is then incorporated into a forwards movement, semi-crouched down doing the arm strokes of the crawl. This is then taken on from passive gliding using the crawl arm strokes and breathing, up to the completely coordinated crawl technique together with breathing. The steps are explained in detail in Chapter 3.5.

The following checklist gives a quick overview of the of a pupil's ability to **breathe** *while swimming. At the same time it also gives tips on further measures to support this learning goal.*

Checklist: Breathing

Partial Learning Goals	Level of Ability yes	no	Comments	Game/ Exercise
1. Keeping the mouth closed/Holding the breath				
• Closing the mouth for a short time				
• Blowing out				
a) on dry land				
b) while in the water				
• Closing the mouth for a period of time				
• Resting the closed mouth on the water				
2. Conscious breathing when not in water				
• Deliberately breathing in and out				
• Deliberate, deep breathing in				
• Deliberate, steady breathing out				
• Holding the breath				
• Rhythmical breathing				
3. Breathing out in chest-deep water				
• Breathing in hip-deep water				
• Breathing in chest-deep water				
• Breathing in deeply in chest-deep water				
• Strong and steady breathing out				
• Rhythmical breathing				
4. Breathing out on the surface of the water				
• Breathing out quickly on the surface of the water				
• Breathing out slowly on the surface of the water				
• Blowing a table tennis ball:				
• A short distance				
• Across the width of the swimming pool				
• Blowing into the water				
5. Breathing out under water				
• Resting the face on the water and breathing out:				
• Breathing out quickly				

Partial Learning Goals	Level of Ability		Comments	Game/ Exercise
	yes	no		
• Breathing out slowly				
• Immersing the face and breathing out:				
• Breathing out quickly				
• Breathing out slowly				
• Rhythmical breathing				
• Head underwater while breathing out				
6. Rhythmical breathing				
• Rhythmical breathing in chest-deep water				
• Rhythmical breathing on the surface of the water				
• Rhythmical breathing, resting the head on the water				
• Rhythmical breathing, head underwater				
7. Rhythmical breathing suitable for the crawl technique				
• Rhythmical breathing at the steps in a press-up position (head is turned to one side when breathing in)				
• Rhythmical breathing while walking crouched				
• Rhythmical breathing (partner pulling)				
• Rhythmical breathing while gliding with a board				
• Rhythmical breathing while using the leg stroke				
8. Overall coordination with breathing				
• Rhythmical breathing and one-sided crawl arm stroke while standing				
• Rhythmical breathing and crawl arm stroke (both arms) while standing				
• Rhythmical breathing and one-sided crawl arm stroke while walking				
• Rhythmical breathing and crawl arm stroke (both arms) while walking				
• Rhythmical breathing and crawl arm stroke while gliding passively				
• Rhythmical breathing and crawl arm stroke when being pushed				
• Overall coordination and breathing				

Figure 31: *Checklist breathing*

2.4 Jumping in and Diving

2.4.1 The Basics of Jumping in and Diving

The ability to *jump in and dive* while swimming for beginners is aimed, above all, to facilitate the following general aims:

* Having fun while jumping in and diving
* Increasing the feeling of safety in the water
* Reducing fear and inhibitions, and promoting self-confidence
* Developing the decision-making ability and willpower
* Gaining various experiences with the movements
* Promoting control of the body
* Learning to follow instructions

Already in the first swimming lessons on *jumping in and diving*, the children have to learn some mandatory safety rules:

* No running jumps or dives may be done because of the high risk of slipping
* Curl the toes round the edge of the pool to avoid slipping
* Only jump in or dive when the surface of the water is free
* Only jump in or dive in when the instructor gives a sign
* No diving headfirst into the learner's pool – this is very dangerous!

Jumping in and diving should also begin with very simple games and exercises, so not to cause stress in over-anxious children. Movement exercises for jumping in and diving stimulate the children's imagination and creativity. This means that many games and exercises should be created as free flowing tasks, so that the children are acquainted with all sorts of movements and become active and creative.

2.4.2 The Methodical Way to Jumping in and Diving

The section on *jumping in and diving* is divided into the following partial learning goals (see Figure 32):

1. Partial Learning Goal: **Hopping and jumping in the water**

The children learn to take their feet off the bottom of the pool for a short while by hopping and jumping

Games and Exercises

→ **Hopping in the water in the learner's pool in a group**
The children form a long row holding hands. They all hop together through the water

→ **Circle and singing games:**
- "Eenie, miny, mo"
- Ring a ring o' roses
- All clap hands
- Show your feet

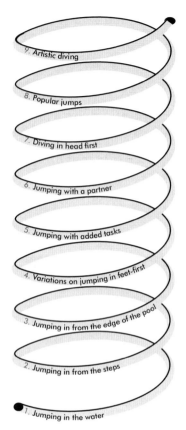

9. Artistic diving

8. Popular jumps

7. Diving in head first

6. Jumping with a partner

5. Jumping with added tasks

4. Variations on jumping in feet-first

3. Jumping in from the edge of the pool

2. Jumping in from the steps

1. Jumping in the water

Figure 32: *Jumping in and Diving*

→ **Hopping around in a circle:**
Everyone hops around in a circle holding hands.

Variations:
- The whole circle hops to the right or left
- hopping with big or little jumps
- jumping up with both legs
- hopping on one leg

→ **Acting games:**
- Hopping like a frog:
Who can hop through the water like a frog?
- Kangaroo hopping:
Everyone hops through the water like kangaroos

- Stork in the reeds:
  Walking like a stork through the water
- Bull in a china shop:
  Walking like a bull through the water
- Guessing the animals:
  Who can move through the water like an animal? The others have to guess the animal

→ **Relay games:**
  - Running relay
  - Hopping relay
  - Obstacle race relay

→ **Jumping and hopping with a partner:**
  One partner holds hands with the other, who tries out different jumps: Jumps in a squatting position, jumps on one leg, turning around while jumping, straddle jumps etc.

  Variations: • one partner tries funny jumps
  - who can splash the most water when jumping?
  - who can jump the highest?
  - hopping in different directions: forwards, backwards, sideways, diagonally

→ **Jumping up and down at the edge of the pool:**
  The children hold on to the edge of the pool and jump up and down in the water.

  Variations: • everyone tries out different jumps
  - everyone holds on with one hand only
  - everyone jumps up and down especially high

→ **Free jumping:**
  Everyone jumps round the learner's pool any way they like.

  Variations: • hopping around on one leg
  - hopping in different directions: forwards, backwards, sideways, diagonally
  - hopping and jumping like animals

2. Partial Learning Goal: **Jumping in from the steps**

The children learn to jump into the water from different heights at the steps.

Games and Exercises

→ **Jumping in from the first step:**

The pupil prepares to do his first jump in with the help of a partner. The partner's help can be reduced gradually.

Variations:
- jumping in from the first step with the help of a partner: the partner helps by supporting with both hands
- jumping in from the first step, whereby the partner's help is gradually reduced:
- one partner holds the other with one hand
- one partner holds the other with the fingers only
- the partner is only there for safety reasons
- jumping from the first step without the help of a partner

→ **Jumping in with added tasks:** Various tasks for jumping in with the goal in mind of "Who can do so and so?"

Variations:
- who can jump in the farthest?
- who can jump in the highest?
- who can jump in in the funniest way?
- who can jump in over a rope?
- who can jump in through a hoop?
- who can jump in in a way that splashes the most?
- who can jump in in a way that splashes the least?

→ **Jumping from the second step:**

With and without the help of the partner – see above
With similar added tasks as above.

→ **Jumping from the third step:**

With and without the help of the partner – see above
With similar extra tasks as above.

→ **Who can jump in over obstacles?**

→ **Picking apples:**

Who can jump up high enough to pick 'apples', balloons, sweets etc., from a rope that is held up in the air?

3. Partial Learning Goal: **Jumping in from the edge of the pool**
The children learn to jump in from the edge of the pool.

Games and Exercises
→ **Jumping in out of the sitting position from the edge of the pool:**
Jumping in from the edge of the pool is first carried out from the sitting position with the help of a partner. The partner's help is then gradually reduced.

Variations: • jumping in with the help of a partner: One partner helps by supporting the other with both hands
• jumping in from the edge of the pool out of the sitting position, while the help of the partner is reduced gradually. The partner only helps with one hand, then only with the finger tips, and finally he is only there for safety reasons
• jumping into the arms of the partner
• jumping in without the help of a partner

→ **Jumping in from the edge of the pool from the squatting position:**
Jumping in from the edge of the pool is carried out from the squatting position first with the help of a partner. The partner's help is gradually reduced.

Variations: • jumping in out of the squatting position with assistance
• reducing the amount of assistance
• without assistance (see above)

→ **Jumping in standing from the edge of the pool:**
Jumping in from the edge of the pool takes place from a standing position with the help of a partner. The partner's help is reduced gradually.

Variations: • jumping in from a standing position with help
• reducing the help
• without help (see above)

4. Partial Learning Goal: **Variations on jumping in feet-first**
The children learn various variations of jumping in from the edge of the pool feet-first.

Games and Exercises

→ **Jumping in from the squatting position:**
Who can pull the legs up close to the body when jumping in?

→ **Walking jumps:** exercises – see above

→ **Jumping up into the air, spinning around and jumping into the water:** exercises – see above

→ **Jumping into the water and doing a forward roll before entering the water:** exercises – see above

→ **Jumping in different directions:** forwards, backwards, sideways: exercises – see above

→ Who can jump in the farthest?

→ Who can jump in the highest?

→ Who can jump in in the funniest way?

→ Who can jump in like a frog?

> *Variations:* • who can jump in like a dolphin?
> • who can jump in like a whale?

5. Partial Learning Goal: Jumping in with added tasks

The children learn to jump in from the edge of the pool with added tasks.

Games and Exercises

→ Who can jump in over or onto a swimming board?

→ Who can jump in over a rope?

→ Who can jump in through a hoop?

→ Jumping in through a hoop and diving underneath the hoop

→ Who can do jump ins with turns?

→ Who can jump in in a way that splashes the most?

→ Who can jump in in a way that splashes the least?

→ **Clown jumps:** Who can jump in in a funny manner like a clown?

6. Partial Learning Goal: **Jumping in with a partner and in a group**

The children learn to jump in with a partner or in a group.

Games and Exercises
→ **Who can create jumps with a partner?**
* foot jumps
* funny jumps
* more adventurous jumps requiring a bit more courage
* piggyback jumps
* handstand jumps etc.

→ **Jumps in small groups:**
Chain reaction:
The children sit with their backs to the water very close to the edge of the pool and link arms with their neighbors. When the first child lets itself fall backwards into the water, the others follow in a "chain reaction".
Bob sleigh run:
The children sit at the edge of the pool with one shoulder pointing in the direction of the water. They sit so close behind each other that they are sitting between the legs of the child behind them and can touch the shoulders of the child in front. The whole group now imagines that it is sitting in a very big bob sleigh and travelling down a bob sleigh course. A slight curve to the left comes (everyone leans slightly to the left), then comes a greater curve to the right (everyone leans to the right) and finally there is a big curve to the left, so that all children fall one after another into the water.

7. Partial Learning Goal: **Diving in headfirst**

The children learn to dive in headfirst from the edge of the pool.

Games and Exercises
→ **Diving headfirst from the steps (the gliding dive)**

Variations: • diving headfirst from the first step
• diving headfirst from the second step
• diving headfirst from the third step

→ Diving headfirst through a hoop:

Variations: • diving over a magic rope
 • diving over the arms of a partner

→ Diving headfirst from the edge of the pool out of a sitting position

Variations: • diving from a deep squatting position
 • diving from a standing position
 • diving head first from the starting block or the 1-m springboard

8. Partial Learning Goal: Popular jumps
The children learn to jump in in ordinary popular ways.

Games and Exercises
→ Variations of jumping in with the feet off the edge of the pool:
 • jumping in from a squatting position
 • jumping in by doing a walking jump
 • straddle and straddle-angle jumps
 • jumping up into the air, spinning around and jumping into the water: exercises – see above
 • jumping into the water, doing a forward roll before entering the water: exercises – see above
 • jumping in different directions – forwards, backwards, sideways: exercises – see above

Photo 8: *Headfirst dive from the edge of the pool*

→ Foot jumps with added tasks:
- who can jump the farthest?
- who can jump the highest?
- who can do the funniest jump?

→ Jumping with the partner or in a group (see above)

→ Foot jump variations from the starting block

→ Foot jump variations from the 3-m springboard

→ Falling forwards off the 1-m springboard

→ Falling forwards off the 3-m springboard

→ Falling backwards off the 3-m springboard or from the tower

9. Partial Learning Goal: **Artistic jumping and diving**
The children learn to jump or dive in artistically.

Games and Exercises
→ Jumping in from the 1-m springboard:
- jumping in feet-first from the 1-m springboard with a run-up
- headfirst dive
- somersaulting forwards, backwards
- dolphin jumps
- reverse somersaults
- twist jumps

→ Jumping from the 3-m springboard and from the tower

*The following checklist allows a quick overview of the pupil's **jumping and diving abilities**. At the same time it also gives tips on more ways to achieve this goal.*

Checklist: Jumping in and Diving

Partial Learning Goals	Level of Ability		Comments	Game/ Exercise
	yes	no		
1. Jumping in the water				
• Hopping while holding hands in a group				
• Hopping while holding hands with a partner				
• Hopping and jumping at the edge of the pool				
• Hopping and jumping freely in hip-deep water				
• Hopping and jumping freely in chest-deep water				
2. Jumping in from the steps				
• Jumping in from the first step of the pool				
a) With the help of a partner				
b) Without the help of a partner				
c) Various types of jumps				
• Jumping from the second step				
a) With the help of a partner				
b) Without the help of a partner				
c) Foot jump variations				
• Jumping from the third step				
a) With the help of a partner				
b) Without the help of a partner				
c) Various types of jumps				
3. Jumping in from the edge of the pool				
• Jumping in out of the sitting position at the edge of the pool				
a) With the help of a partner				
b) With ensured safety				
c) Various types of jumps				
• Jumping in out of the squatting position				
a) With the help of a partner				
b) With ensured safety				
c) Various types of jumps				
• Jumping in from a standing position				
a) With the help of a partner				
b) With ensured safet				
c) Without the help of a partner				

Partial Learning Goals	Level of Ability		Comments	Game/ Exercise
	yes	no		
4. Variations on jumping in feet-first				
• Stretched up (star) jump				
• Squat jump				
• Walking jump				
• Jump with turns around the longitudinal axis of the body				
• Jump with turns around the latitudinal axis of the body				
• Jump backwards				
• Additional variations				
5. Jumping in with added tasks				
• Jumping in over/onto a swimming board				
• Jump in over a rope				
• Jump in through a hoop				
• Jump in through a hoop and dive under				
6. Jumping with a partner/in a group				
• Jumping in with two people feet-first				
• Piggyback jump				
• Chain reaction				
• Bob sleigh run				
7. Diving headfirst				
• Headfirst dive from the steps				
a) from the first step				
b) from the second step				
c) from the third step				
• Headfirst dive from the steps through a hoop				
a) from the first step				
b) from the second step				
c) from the third step				
• Jumping in from the edge of the pool				
a) out of the sitting position				
b) from a squatting position				
c) from a standing position				

Partial Learning Goals	Level of Ability		Comments	Game/Exercise
	yes	no		
• Headfirst dive from the starting block				
a) out of a sitting position				
b) from a squatting position				
c) from a standing position				
8. Popular jumps				
• Foot jump variations				
a) Squatting position jump				
b) Walking jump				
c) Straddle jump				
• Jumping and twisting				
• Jumping into the water, doing forward roll before entering the water				
• a) Roll in				
b) Somersault forwards				
c) Somersault backwards				
Letting oneself fall				
a) from the 1-m springboard				
b) from the 2-m springboard				
c) from the 3-m springboard				
9. Artistic Jumping	1 m	3 m		Tower
Ordinary jumping				
Diving headfirst				
Forward somersaults				
Backward somersaults				
Dolphin jumps				
Reverse somersaults				
Twist jumps				

Figure 33: *Checklist Jumping in and Diving*

2.5 Floating

2.5.1 The Basics of Floating

Everything immersed in water experiences buoyancy. Buoyancy (as per Archimedes law) counteracts gravity and is therefore as large as the volume of water displaced. In simpler terms we can say that an object that is immersed in water seems to lose as much weight as the amount of water it displaces.

Dependent on the density of an object; it can float on the water (the density or specific weight is less than that of water: e.g., cork, wood, ball), it can glide in the water (the density is the same as that of the water: e.g., a balloon, which is filled with water) or it can sink (e.g., a stone, because its density is greater than that of water). The human body also experiences this buoyancy. As the specific weight of the human body is not much different from that of water, nearly every human can swim in water. He does not need a lot of strength to stay on the surface of the water. Those learning to swim need to experience this buoyancy, i.e. they have to feel that their body stays on the surface of the water even without movement – it floats.

Initially children are not used to the horizontal position adopted when floating. Children lift their heads out of the water to orient themselves. This reflex must be suppressed. To reach the ideal position in the water while swimming, the head must rest on the water. For beginners it is difficult to balance the body correctly in this position in the water. Changing to a standing position from a swimming position also causes difficulties initially. Beginner swimmers are unsure how to find solid ground with their feet when coming out of the horizontal position in the water. Children quickly become anxious when they cannot feel ground under their feet anymore. Therefore they have to learn – as must anxious adult beginner swimmers – how to return to a safe standing position from the gliding position. The following tips can show the right way to do so: "Draw the legs up close to the body and put the feet onto the ground."

2.5.2 Practicing Floating

First of all we will go through games and exercises, which get you floating without consciously doing it. Then we introduce games, which help you to deliberately float. With the help of a partner, floating freely can be practiced by letting parts of the body float.

The section on *floating* is divided into the following partial learning goals:

1. Partial Learning Goal: Experiencing floating without consciously doing it

Children learn to float without consciously doing it by playing games.

Games and exercises:

→ Practicing floating without consciously doing it (involuntarily) using circle and singing games:
  - "Show us your feet"
  - "Ring a ring o' roses"

→ Practicing involuntary floating using running and catching games:
  - Chain catch
  - Duck hunting
  - ABC-catching
  - Magic mouse, etc.

→ Practicing involuntary floating using relay games:
  - Running relay
  - Obstacle relay
  - Carry relay
  - Hanger-on relay
  - Push and pull relay

→ Practicing involuntary floating using small ball games:
  - Passing the ball in a circle
  - Tiger ball
  - Party ball

→ Practicing involuntary floating using underwater diving games:
  see section on underwater diving

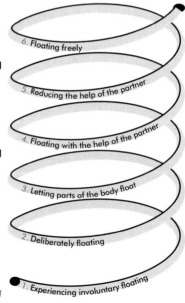

6. Floating freely

5. Reducing the help of the partner

4. Floating with the help of the partner

3. Letting parts of the body float

2. Deliberately floating

1. Experiencing involuntary floating

Figure 34: *Floating*

2. Partial Learning Goal: **Deliberately floating**

The children experience the buoyancy of the water with different objects and with their own body.

→ Observing various objects as they float:
Pushing various objects under water and observing their behavior: e.g. balls, hoops, swimming boards, diving stones etc.

→ Making the children aware that some objects can float naturally:
Talking about the different floating behavior of balls, balloons, swimming boards, diving hoops and other toys and creating awareness of the phenomenon of buoyancy.

→ Making the children aware of the buoyancy of the human body:
"The children find out how the human body behaves in water":

Variations: • experiencing floating while standing
 • experiencing floating while in a deep squatting position and in other positions
 • experiencing floating while breathing in deeply

3. Partial Learning Goal: **Letting parts of the body float**

The children experience consciously parts of the body float.

Games and exercises:

→ Letting parts of the body float while standing:
Going into a squatting position in chest-deep water so that the shoulders are under water. The arms can now float up without effort.

→ Floating while lying on the stomach (forward press-up position):
The hands support the body on the bottom of the pool or on a step. After breathing in deeply, observe how the body floats.

Variations: • moving the stretched-out body alternately back and forth
 • moving forwards on hands while on the steps or on the bottom of the pool

→ Consciously, breathe in and out slowly. While doing this, observe:
 • how the body sinks down slowly when breathing out
 • how the body comes into a floating position when slowly breathing in (feeling how the trunk of the body and the legs surface).

→ **Taking the hands off the ground while experimenting:**
Supporting the body with the fingertips only. Support the body with one hand only (changing hands). Take both hands off the ground for a short time. Immerse the head (resting the face on the water), having already put the shoulders under the surface of the water.

→ **Floating while lying on the back (supine press-up position):**
Support the body with the hands placed on either side of the buttocks on the bottom of the pool or on a step. Stretch the toes out of the water. The lower legs surface and float.

Variations: • the shoulders and the back of the head rest on the water.
• the water laps round the ears.
• the body is supported by the fingertips only.
• take the fingers off the ground briefly.

→ **Floating at the edge of the pool:**
With slight modification, the exercises at the steps can also be practiced easily at the edge of the pool. Exercises and variations are as above.

4. Partial Learning Goal: Floating with the help of the partner
The children let their bodies float with the help of a partner.

Games and exercises:
→ **Floating in a circle:**
The children stand in a circle holding hands. Every second child is now allowed to rest on the water, the others supporting them safely.

Variations: • on the stomach
• on the back
• the children are now allowed to kick with their legs
• play a game such as "Ring a ring o' roses"

→ **Floating with the help of a partner:**
One partner takes his legs off the ground, with the other holding and supporting him.

Variations: • on the stomach
• on the back
• changing the position from the front to the back without standing (lateral rotation)
• partner supports with one arm only

5. Partial Learning Goal: **Reducing the help of the partner**

The children find out that their bodies will also surface and float without the help of a partner.

Games and exercises:

→ **Floating first of all with the support of the partner.** This help is reduced gradually in small steps. One partner takes the legs of the ground, the other holds him and supports him with both hands, with one hand, with the fingertips only and finally only to offer support if needed.

  Variations: • on the stomach
  • on the back
  • changing the position from the front to the back without standing (lateral rotation)

6. Partial Learning Goal: **Floating freely**

The children should be able to let the body float freely.

Games and exercises:

→ **The squatting jelly fish:**
  Breathe in deeply, going into the squatting position, with the legs drawn close up to the body, and with the arms around the knees. The body can now float freely.

→ **The stretched jelly fish:**
  Breathe in deeply, lying stretched out on the water.

  Variations: • on the front
  • on the back
  • either on the stomach or on the back with arms and legs stretched out

→ **The diving jelly fish:**
  Breathe in and then dive downwards. Then come to the surface again.

→ **Submarine:**
  Climb down the rungs of the ladder that leads into the pool, a pole or the legs of the partner. Then let go and come to the surface again.

*The following checklist allows a quick overview of a pupil's ability to **float**. At the same time it also gives tips on more way to achieve this learning goal.*

Checklist: Floating

Partial Learning Goals	Level of Ability		Comments	Game/ Exercise
	yes	no		
1. Experience involuntary floating				
• In circle and singing games				
• In running and catching games				
• In relay games				
• In ball games				
• In games using equipment				
2. Deliberately floating				
• Experiencing the buoyancy of objects				
• Recognizing the buoyancy factor with different objects				
• Experiencing how their own bodies can float				
3. Letting parts of the body float				
• Letting the arms surface and float while in shoulder-deep water				
• Letting the legs surface and float while in a press-up position at the steps				
a) front position				
b) back position				
• Letting the body surface and float at the edge of the pool				
a) front position				
b) back position				
4. Floating with the help of a partner				
• Floating in a circle				
a) front position				
b) back position				
• Partner supports the other with both hands while he floats				
a) front position				
b) back position				
• Partner supports other with one hand				
a) front position				
b) back position				

Partial Learning Goals	Level of Ability		Comments	Game/ Exercise
	yes	no		
5. Reducing the help of the partner				
• Partner supports				
• With one hand				
• With one finger				
• Without contact (except to ensure safety only)				
a) front position				
b) back position				
6. Floating freely				
• The squatting jelly fish				
• The stretched out jelly fish				
• The diving jelly fish				

Figure 35: *Floating Checklist*

2.6   Gliding

2.6.1   The Basics of Gliding

Gliding plays a very central role in getting used to the water and swimming for beginners. Gliding freely is the main basis of learning swimming techniques. The ability to glide is a necessary part of the learning process for introducing swimming styles and for the techniques of starts and turns.

Games and exercises that require the pupil to stretch his body out in the water are very good preparation for gliding. The pre-requisites for gliding are to have experienced of state of static floating. When the pupil has already experienced this, the non-swimmer can progress to dynamic floating – gliding. During this phase, taking the arms and legs off the ground, gliding when the body is in the stretched position and the automatic linking of breathing with gliding can be learned methodically as the first steps towards coordination. When the beginner has mastered gliding, he has taken an important step in the process of going from being a non-swimmer to being a swimmer.

One problem is when trying to stand up out of the gliding position. The children have to learn to draw their legs up close to the body, when in the gliding position, and then to put them down again vertically onto the ground. Slipping on the ground can lead to traumatic experiences. Therefore standing up should be introduced as a part of gliding.

2.6.2   Learning to Glide

Gliding can be introduced with different target groups (babies, toddlers, anxious children and those with various handicaps) very early on via "passive gliding". This is done by the (adult) helper first pulling the pupil along close to his body. It is advantageous to start with the child lying on its back, as this allows easier breathing and the child also feels more secure by putting its head onto the helper's shoulder. While doing this, the head is actively drawn back which promotes a comfortable position in the water when on the back. Later on, the helper can simply submerge his shoulders deeper under the water so that now the child's head is supported by the water and the shoulder. This is good preparation for the stage when the head is supported only by the water. When the helper pulls with stretched arms, this is the first stage towards the helper releasing altogether. Other games and exercises with equipment like swimming boards, pull-buoys etc., also prepare the pupil for active gliding.

Photo 9: *Gliding in the partner's wake*

An important step in going from passive to active gliding is gliding in the partner's wake. First the child, floating on his back and held close to the body of the helper, is pulled through the water. Now the helper can let the child go. Walking backwards creates a so-called wake, which allows the child to be pulled across the width of the pool without body contact.

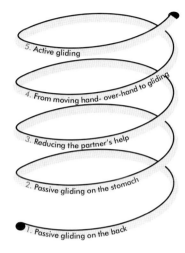

5. Active gliding

4. From moving hand- over-hand to gliding

3. Reducing the partner's help

2. Passive gliding on the stomach

1. Passive gliding on the back

Figure 36: *Gliding*

The section on *gliding* is divided into the following partial learning goals:

1. Partial Learning Goal: **Passive gliding on the back**

The children come into the gliding position by being pulled along while lying on the back.

Photo 10: *Pulling a child along close to the helper's body*

Games and exercises:

→ **Pulling the partner along on his back and held close to the body** (hold under the armpits and let the head rest on the shoulders).

→ **Pulling the partner along on his back**: this time the person pulling has his shoulders at the same height as the water so that the head of the person being pulled comes closer and closer to the surface of the water.

• Pulling the partner along on his back with the helper's arms stretched out.

• Pulling the partner along on his back on a swimming bar or a swimming board.

2. Partial Learning Goal: Passive gliding on the stomach
The children come into the gliding position by being pulled along while lying on the stomach.

Games and exercises:

→ Pulling the partner along on his stomach, close to the helper.

→ Pulling the partner along on his stomach with the stretched arms of the helper.

→ Pulling the partner along on his stomach on a swimming bar or a swimming board.

3. Partial Learning Goal: Reducing the partner's help
The children gradually reduce their dependency on their partner in steps.

Games and exercises:

→ **Pulling the partner along on his back** by the arms stretched out.

→ **Pulling the partner along on his back** with the arms stretched out , letting go for a moment and letting the partner glide a short distance in the other partner's wake.

Variations: • the partner pulls the swimming bar and then lets go.
• the partner pulls the swimming board and then lets go.
• pulling the partner along and letting him go so that he glides alone without a swimming board.

→ Gliding in a partner's wake over a longer distance.

→ Pulling the partner along on his stomach with stretched-out arms and gliding in a partner's wake.

→ Pulling the partner along on his stomach with stretched-out arms and letting the partner glide a short distance alone, to the edge of the pool or to the steps.

Variations: see above

→ Gliding in a partner's wake over a longer distance while lying on the stomach

→ Gliding towards the partner (e.g., from the steps) and being pulled along further on the back or the stomach.

→ Increasing the distance that was glided alone

→ Gliding alone towards the edge of the pool or the stairs.

→ Rafting:
The children form an alleyway. One child – the raft – lies and floats at the beginning of this alleyway and is pushed through it by the others.

Variations: • rafting while lying on the stomach
• rafting while lying on the back
• rafting under the surface of the water
• rafting through the alleyway and then gliding further

→ The torpedo game:
In a group of three, two children hold hands. One child lies on the hands and is then thrown in a forward direction like a torpedo after being swung forward and backwards.

Variations: • torpedo – while lying on the stomach
• torpedo – while lying on the back
• "Torpedo stations" are placed in all 4 corners of the learner's pool. The torpedoes are thrown from one station to another.

→ **Fish over the table:**
The children form a corridor and hold hands with the partner opposite. One child lies at the beginning of this alleyway on the hands and is transported by gentle up- and down movements of the hands over the 'table' to the other side.

Variations: • the fish is thrown over the 'table' quite high up
• the fish somersaults, i.e., does a forward roll etc., at the end
• "flying" over the table on the back

4. Partial Learning Goal: From moving hand-over-hand to gliding
The children progress from moving hand-over-hand to gliding.

Games and exercises:

→ **Moving along the edge of the pool hand-over-hand:**
First, one of the children moves hand-over-hand along the edge of the pool with a partner supporting him.

Variations: • the child moves hand-over-hand with both hands along the edge of the pool
• the child moves along the edge of the pool using only one hand
• the child moves hand-over-hand along the edge of the pool and every now and then glides a short distance.

→ **Moving hand-over-hand on a rope/line:**
First one child moves hand-over-hand along a rope with a partner who supports him.

Variations: • the child moves hand-over-hand with both hands
• the child moves with only one hand
• the child moves hand-over-hand and every now and then glides a short distance

→ Moving along a chain of partners:
One child moves hand-over-hand along a chain of partners, from one to another.

Variation: • the partners stand close to each other
• the partners increase the distance between each other

5. Partial Learning Goal: **Active gliding**

The children glide along on their own after pushing themselves off from the edge of the pool.

Games and exercises:

→ Pushing oneself off from the side of the pool and gliding while lying on the stomach:
The children push themselves off the steps while lying on their stomachs and glide.

Variations: • gliding towards a partner
• increasing the distance between the partners
• gliding without the help of a partner
• gliding with a swimming bar
• gliding with a swimming board
• gliding freely

→ Pushing off from the side of the pool while lying on the stomach and gliding:

Variations: see above

→ Pushing off from a partner while lying on the stomach and gliding:

Variations: see above

→ Pushing off from the edge of the pool and gliding:

Variations: see above

→ Pushing off while lying on one's stomach after a headfirst jump and then gliding

→ Pushing off from the side of the pool and gliding while lying on one's back:
The children push themselves off the steps while lying on the back and glide towards a partner.

Variations: • increasing the distance between partners
• gliding without the help of a partner
• additional variations see above (gliding while lying on the stomach)

→ Who can glide the farthest?

Variations: • gliding while lying on the stomach, with or without a swimming board

• gliding while lying on the back with or without a swimming board

→ Gliding in a circle:
"Ring a ring o' roses" as mentioned above. When the circle has gained enough speed, the children lying on the water let go and continue to glide along on their own.

→ The flying fish

→ Gliding stroke

→ Gliding and at the same time turning from lying on the stomach to lying on the back

The following checklist allows a quick overview of a pupil's ability to **glide**. At the same time it also gives tips on further ways to achieve this learning goal.

Checklist Gliding

Partial Learning Goals	Level of Ability		Comments	Game/ Exercise
	yes	no		
1. Passive gliding on the back				
• Being pulled along while lying on the back close to the person pulling				
• Being pulled along while lying on the back close to the person pulling close to the surface of the water				
• Being pulled along while lying on the back with stretched out arms of the person pulling				
• Being pulled along while lying on the back on a swimming bar or board				
2. Passive gliding on the stomach				
• Being pulled along while lying on the stomach close to the person pulling				
• Being pulled along while lying on the stomach, close to the person pulling and close to the surface of the water				
• Being pulled while lying on the stomach with stretched arms of the person pulling				
• Being pulled along while lying on the stomach on a swimming bar or board				
3. Reducing the amount of the partner's help				
• Being pulled along with stretched out arms while lying on the back				
• Being pulled along with stretched out arms while lying on the back and letting go for a few moments				
• Gliding in a partner's wake				
• Being pulled along while lying on the stomach and letting go for a few moments				
a) with a swimming board				
b) without a swimming board				
• Gliding in a partner's wake				
• Being pulled along and then gliding to the steps or the edge of the pool				

Partial Learning Goals	Level of Ability		Comments	Game/ Exercise
	yes	no		
• a) with a swimming board				
b) without a swimming board				
• Gliding towards a partner and being pulled along further				
a) with a swimming board				
b) without a swimming board				
4. From moving hand-over-hand to gliding				
• Moving hand-over-hand along the edge of the pool				
• Moving hand-over-hand along a rope				
• Moving hand-over-hand along a partner chain				
5. Active gliding				
a) Stomach position				
• Pushing off from the steps and gliding towards a partner				
a) with a swimming board				
b) without a swimming board				
• Pushing off from the side of the pool and gliding towards a partner				
a) with a swimming board				
b) without a swimming board				
• Pushing off from the steps/side of the pool and gliding freely				
a) with a swimming board				
b) without a swimming board				
• Pushing off from the side of the pool when sitting on the edge of the pool and then go on gliding				
a) with a swimming board				
b) without a swimming board				
• Jumping in headfirst and gliding				
a) from the steps				
b) from the edge of the pool				

Partial Learning Goals	Level of Ability		Comments	Game/ Exercise
	yes	no		
a) Back position				
• Pushing off from the steps and gliding				
a) with a swimming board				
b) without a swimming board				
• Pushing off from the side of the pool and gliding				
a) with a swimming board				
b) without a swimming board				
• Pushing off from the edge of the pool and gliding				
a) with a swimming board				
b) without a swimming board				
• Gliding Distance				
a) lying on the front: X m				
b) lying on the back: X				

Figure 37: *Checklist Gliding*

2.7 Elementary Swimming Movements – How to Move in the Water

2.7.1 The Basics of Elementary Swimming Movements

The section "Elementary swimming movements – how to move in the water" is a very important and extensive area of swimming for beginners that goes much further than the beginner's area. As before, the sections overlap each other. Thus, many games and exercises can be used for a number of sub-sections and partial learning goals. In particular, the elementary swimming movements are meant to teach various movements, on which the learning of swimming techniques and other techniques of swimming (starts, turns, catching and throwing, jumping in, diving, etc) can be built upon.

In general, the goal of *elementary swimming movements* – how to move in the water, can be explained as follows:

Various experiences of movements in, at, and under the water are gained in a playful and creative manner.

Additional goals are:
- Experiencing water pressure and thermal characteristics
- Experiencing water resistance
- Keeping or recovering the balance
- Learning about buoyancy and the ways of moving forward

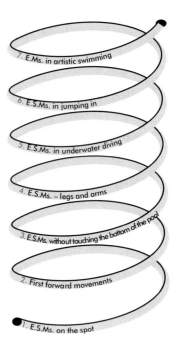

Figure 38: *Elementary swimming movements – how to move in the water*

2.7.2   The Methodical Way

The section *"elementary swimming movements – how to move in the water"* is divided into various partial learning goals:

The following main partial learning goals give structure to the area of "elementary swimming movements and how to move in the water":

1. **Elementary swimming movements on the spot with the feet touching the bottom of the pool**
2. **Initial forward swimming movements with the feet touching the bottom of the pool**
3. **Elementary swimming movements without touching the bottom**
4. **First swimming movement without touching the bottom of the pool using elementary movements of the legs and arms**
5. **Beginning with the elementary swimming movements of diving and moving up through the "First Steps in Diving" to scuba-diving**

6. Beginning with elementary swimming movements of jumping in up through ordinary popular jumping in and diving actions to doing competitive and high-diving
7. Beginning with simple circle and singing games through how to move in the water with music to artistic and synchronized swimming

1. Elementary swimming movements on the spot with the feet touching the bottom of the pool

The following goals are to be achieved in this partial learning goal:

- Keeping one's balance in knee-deep water
- Keeping one's balance in hip-deep water
- Keeping one's balance in shoulder-deep water

Games and exercises:

a) *Individual exercises:*

→ Standing in calm water (with or without the help of a partner):
The child tries to stand in calm water and to keep his balance.

→ Standing in moving water:
One partner stands on both feet in the water. Another partner tries to cause turbulence in the water (e.g., by moving the arms or the whole body). The partner standing tries to keep or recover his balance.

Variations: • keeping the balance with closed eyes
• a number of partners cause turbulence
• standing on one leg and keeping the balance
• using the arms to keep balance in the water

→ Keeping the balance in an eddy:
The children hold hands and form a circle. They begin to move in a circle so that their movements create an eddy. When the eddy is strong enough everyone stands still and tries to keep his balance.

Variations: • keeping one's balance on both legs
• keeping one's balance on one leg
• keeping one's balance with closed eyes

→ **Keeping the balance in waves:**
One part of the group stands at the edge of the pool, holding on with both hands and creating waves by moving forwards and backwards together. The rest of the group stands in the waves and tries to keep their balance:

Variations: • keeping the balance on both legs
• keeping the balance on one leg
• keeping the balance with closed eyes

b) *Exercises with a partner:*

→ **Making the partner lose his balance:**
One partner tries to make the other lose his balance by causing waves or turbulence.

→ **Tug-of-war:**
Two partners stand facing each other, holding each other by the right hand. Each tries to pull the other to his side.

Variations: • pulling with the left hand
• pulling with both hands

→ **Pushing fight:**
Two partners stand facing each other about 1 m apart, holding hands at the height of their shoulders. Each partner tries to make the other lose his balance. The balance is lost, when one partner takes one foot off the ground.

Variations: • pushing with one hand
• pushing or giving way with both hands
• both partners push back to back
• two groups stand back to back and try to push the other group to the other side.

→ **Cockfighting:**
Two children stand facing each other and cross their arms in front of their chests. They hop towards each other, trying to make the other lose his balance.

Variations: • hopping on one leg
• fighting against a number of "cocks"

c) Group Exercises:

→ **Sea snake:**
A group of 4-7 children form a long sea snake by holding each other by the shoulders. The sea snake then moves in different ways through the pool.

Variations: • a number of sea snakes meet and greet each other
                • the sea snakes try to surround each other
                • sea snake race

→ **Head and tail:**
A group of 4-7 children forms a long sea snake by holding each other on the shoulders. The head of the sea snake then tries to catch its tail.

→ **Tug-of-war:**
Two teams of equal strength stand facing each other holding a rope. Each team tries to pull the other to its own side.

Variation: • tug-of-war without a rope: Two groups of 3-8 children stand facing each other. The first members of the group hold hands. The others stand behind them and form a line by placing their hands on the hips of the person in front. Each group tries to pull the other to its side.

→ **Pulling fight in groups:**
Two groups stand facing each other. Each member presses his left hand against that of the person opposite and his right hand against that of another person. The whole group is connected like a zipper. Finally, each group tries to push the other group away.

2. Initial forward swimming movements with the feet touching the bottom of the pool

This partial learning goal aims to achieve the following goals:

• Experiencing water resistance
• Experiencing buoyancy and forward movement

Games and exercises

a) *Making simple forward movements in the water*

→ **Walking in a group:**
The children hold hands and walk round in a circle

Variations: • everyone moves behind each other like a long snake
• walking through the water with a partner

→ **Walking alone through the water**
The children walk on their own through the water unassisted.

Variations: • running, hopping, jumping
• moving forwards, backwards or sideways

→ **The children move through the water like animals.** They can give their imagination free rein.

Variations: • hopping like frogs
• jumping like kangaroos
• galloping like horses
• trampling like elephants
• walking like a stork, etc.

b) *Running and catching games:*
The children can have fun achieving the goals mentioned above by playing the following games:

→ **Catching in pairs**

→ **Getting caught and getting freed again**

→ **Magic mouse**

→ **Chain-catching**

→ **"Who is afraid of the big white shark?"**

→ **"Fisherman, fisherman, how deep is the water?"**

→ **Additional catching games** can be made up by the instructor or his pupils

c) *Circle and Singing games:*

→ "Eenie, miny, mo"

→ "Show your feet"

→ "I'm going to wash that man right out of my hair"

→ Come with us, run away

d) *Complex forward movement*

→ **Jumping over obstacles:**
The children go over different obstacles in the learner's pool (hoops under water, hoops on the surface of the water, slalom bars, etc.)

Variations: • who can get over the obstacles in the most imaginative way?
• varying the obstacles
• hurdling obstacles in the form of a relay race

→ **Carrying relays:**
The children carry various objects in a relay, e.g. a swimming board is used as a "baton" and is passed on to the next child.

Variations: • pull-buoy, ball as baton
• various objects are used as baton
• carrying and collecting relay: The first child carries an object, e.g., a swimming board; the next child fetches and adds a ball to the load; the third another object (pull-buoy or diving weight as a baton, etc.,) until the fifth child has reached the goal, carrying five objects.

→ **Walking in the water:**
Different ways of moving forward can be practiced by giving simple tasks. Movement in different directions can be tried out: walking forwards, backwards or sideways.

Variations: • walking with and without moving the arms
• walking with different arm strokes (alternating, simultaneous)
• walking and doing arm strokes with different positions of the hands (cf., Chapter 3.2).

→ **Relays:**
Running relays: running forwards, backwards or sideways
Carrying and collecting relays: see above

e) *Ball games*
→ Games with little balls:
Hunter's ball, tiger ball, catching ball, Volkerball.

→ Goal-related ball games:
Water polo, water basketball, water football

→ Rebounding ball games:
Water volleyball, water tennis, etc.

3. Elementary swimming movements without touching the bottom

The following goals are to be achieved in this partial learning goal:

- Experiencing buoyancy and forward movement in water of varying depths while lying on the back or stomach.

Games and exercises

a) *Passive gliding while lying on the back*
→ Pulling the partner along lying on the back, close to the body of the helper

Photo 11: *Passive gliding lying on the back, close to the body of the helper*

→ Pulling the partner along lying on the back, with arms stretched out

→ Pulling the partner along lying on the back, with a swimming bar

→ Pulling the partner along lying on the back, with a swimming board

b) *Turning from the back onto the stomach*

As some people, especially nervous children, are afraid of or hesitant about lying on the water on their stomachs, gliding on their backs first is good preparation for gliding on their stomachs. When the child is used to gliding by being pulled on its back, it can be turned over onto its stomach just before reaching the edge of the pool after being pulled backwards. The child can then hold onto the edge of the pool with its hands and stretch forward in the manner required for gliding on its stomach. In this way the child will have lost its fear of lying on the big, unknown area of water. In several small steps, the time required to turn over from its back onto its stomach, and hence the distance to the wall, can be increased.

c) *Passive gliding while lying on the stomach*

→ **Pulling the partner along, close to the body of the helper**

→ **Pulling the partner along with arms stretched out**

→ **Pulling the partner along with a swimming bar**

→ **Pulling the partner along with a swimming board**

d) *Reducing the amount of help from the partner*

→ Gliding in a partner's wake (lying on the back or the stomach)

→ One partner pulls the other along as far as just before the edge of the pool. He then lets go so that the other partner can glide to the edge (on his back or stomach)

→ The distance that the partner glides alone is continuously increased

→ One partner glides towards the other, who then pulls him further (on his back or front)

→ Increasing the distance

→ Gliding towards the steps/edge of the pool (on his back or front)

→ Who can glide the longest distance?

→ Torpedo game

→ Rafting

e) *Moving hand-over-hand*
→ Moving hand-over-hand along the edge of the pool

→ Moving hand-over-hand along a rope

→ Moving along a partner chain

f) *Active gliding*
→ From the steps (both with or without a swimming board)

→ From the wall

→ From the edge of the pool

→ From a sitting position

→ From a squatting position

→ Gliding from the jump

→ From the starting dive (cf., Chapter 2.6)

4. First swimming movements without touching the bottom of the pool using elementary leg and arm movements

Goal: Increasing the gliding distance using elementary movements:

- of the legs
- of the arms
- of arms and legs
- overall coordination

a) Gliding and elementary leg movements
By using elementary leg movements, the gliding position can be stabilized and the distance increased. These elementary leg movements can first be practiced and learned during passive gliding (being pulled along by the partner) before proceeding to moving forward on one's own. Elementary leg movements can be introduced in the following structured steps:

→ **Being pulled along while lying on the back and carrying out elementary leg movements:**
While being pulled along on its back, a child can actively assist the forward movement by carrying out "paddling movements" with its legs. These movements can be assisted initially by using flippers. Thus the children quickly learn the first active "swimming movements".

Variations: • with a swimming bar/swimming board and flippers
• with flippers
• without aids

→ **Being pulled along while lying on the stomach and carrying out elementary leg movements:** see above

Variations: • with a swimming bar/swimming board and flippers
• with flippers
• without aids

→ **Reducing the amount of help from the partner:**
The child is pulled along on its back by its partner who lets go for a short moment so that the child can glide on by itself in the partner's wake. The distance the child glides on its own is gradually increased.

Variations: • lying on the back
• with a swimming bar/swimming board and flippers
• with flippers
• without aids
Variations: • lying on the stomach
• with a swimming bar/swimming board and flippers
• with flippers
• without aids

→ **Gliding independently on the back and elementary leg movements:**
When pushing themselves off from the steps or the wall of the pool, children can only glide a certain distance, which can be actively increased using elementary leg kicking movements.

Variations: • with a swimming bar/swimming board and flippers
• with flippers
• without aids

→ **Gliding independently while lying on the stomach and elementary leg movements:**
When pushing themselves off from the stairs or the wall children now can glide a distance, which can be actively increased using elementary leg kicking movements.

Variations: • with a swimming bar/swimming board and flippers
• with flippers
• without aids

b) **Gliding and elementary arm movements**
1. Gliding and elementary arm movements while on the back
→ **Paddling movements while on the back:**
First one partner pushes the child through the water on his back while supporting his hips. At the same time the child being pushed assists the forward movement by paddling with the hands.

Variations: • one partner pushes or holds the other's hips
• gliding on the back with a pull-buoy
• reducing the amount of help from the partner
• gliding without aids

→ **Moving the hands sideways:**
First one partner pushes the child through the water on his back while supporting his hips. At the same time the child assists the forward movement by paddling sideways with his hands.

Variations: • partner pushes or holds the hips
• gliding on the back with a pull-buoy
• reducing the amount of help from the partner
• gliding without aids

→ **Stroke movements:**
While being pushed through the water the child performs arm strokes with both arms at the same time.

Variations: • see above

→ **Stroke movements with one arm after another:**
While being pushed through the water the child moves the arms alternately

Variations: • see above

→ Further development of simultaneous arm strokes for the breaststroke on the back

→ Further development of alternating arm strokes when lying on the back leading to the backstroke crawl

2. *Gliding and elementary arm movements when lying on the stomach*

→ **First stroke movements with alternate arms:**
Elementary movements by using the arms alternately leading to the crawl stroke.

→ **Paddling movements when lying on the stomach:**
First of all one partner pushes the child on his stomach through the water while supporting the child at the hips. In the meanwhile the child assists the forward movement by paddling with the hands.

> *Variations:* • partner pushes or holds the hips
> • gliding while lying on the front with a pull-buoy
> • reducing the amount of help from the partner
> • gliding without aids

→ **Stroke movements with alternate arms:**
The paddling movements done lying on the stomach can be converted into stroke movements with alternate arms by employing a number of additional motions.

→ **Further development of the stroke movements with alternate arms leading to the crawl:**
The instructor can set tasks that train the following points of the crawl through experimentation:
• Rhythm: try to use the arms with a regular rhythm!
• Swinging phase: observe how the arms swing forward when practicing this movement out of the water!
• Stroke phase: how can the arm and the hand be pulled through the water so that there is the greatest possible forward movement?
• Pressure phase: see above
• Position of the hands: try to move your arms through the water with your hands in different positions! (cf., Chapter 3.2)

→ **Elementary stroke movements using both arms simultaneously:**
Elementary movements using both arms simultaneously lead to the breaststroke or the butterfly stroke.

→ **Stroke movements using both arms simultaneously:**
First of all, a partner pushes the child on its stomach through the water while supporting the child at the hips. In the meanwhile the child supports the forward movement by using both hands simultaneously.

Variations:
- partner pushes or holds the hips
- gliding while lying on the stomach with a pull-buoy
- reducing the amount of help from the partner
- without aids

→ Further development of the stroke movements with both arms simultaneously leads towards the breaststroke (or butterfly stroke)

c) Elementary steps towards total coordination (without breathing)
1. Alternating arms strokes with the while lying on the stomach (crawl)

→ **Alternating arm strokes, legs dangling**

→ **Alternating arm strokes, deliberate leg movements**

→ **Alternating arm strokes, increased use of the legs**

→ **Alternating kicking movements with the legs, adding arm movements**

→ **Coordination of regular and simultaneous arm strokes together with the kicking movements**

2. Alternating arm strokes while lying on the back (backstroke crawl) (method as explained above while lying on the stomach).

3. Simultaneous strokes with both arms while lying on the back (breaststroke on the back)

→ **Doing a number of arm strokes and adding a leg kick every now and then**

→ **Doing a number of arm strokes and increasing the number of leg kicks**

→ **Doing a number of leg kick movements and adding an arm stroke every now and then**

→ **Doing a number of leg kick movements and increasing the number of arm strokes**

→ One leg kick movement per arm stroke

→ Coordinating the arm strokes and kicking movements together

4. *Simultaneous strokes with both arms while lying on the stomach (breaststroke)*
   (method as explained above while lying on the back)

e) Breathing
→ Exhaling into the water

→ Breathing rhythmically

→ Breathing technique as for the first swimming stroke chosen:
   Crawl stroke: breathing sideways
   Breaststroke: lifting the head while breathing (with and without the help of a partner) (see Chapter 2.3 *Breathing*)

f) Total *coordination* and *breathing* for the first swimming technique chosen
→ Rhythmical breathing

→ Coordinating breathing and kicking

→ Coordinating breathing and arm strokes

→ Overall coordination and breathing

→ First swimming technique chosen (see Chapter 3.5)

5. **Beginning with the elementary swimming movements of diving and moving up through "First steps in diving" to scuba-diving**
→ Diving instructions for swimming beginners: see Chapter 2.2 *underwater diving*

→ First Diving Steps:
   First diving steps with equipment (goggles, snorkel and flippers) can be practiced methodically in small steps. The following process is suggested:
   • Swimming and diving with flippers
   • Swimming and diving with goggles
   • Swimming and diving with snorkel

- Swimming and diving with goggles and snorkel
- Games and exercises using all the above equipment
- Snorkeling

6. **Beginning with elementary swimming movements of jumping in up through ordinary popular jumping in and diving actions to doing competitive diving to sport and high-diving**

→ Jumping in instructions for beginner swimmers:
see Chapter 2.4: *jumping in and diving*

→ Ordinary popular diving

→ Sport and high-diving

7: **Beginning with games played in a simple circle and songs and how to move in the water to music to artistic and synchronized swimming**

→ Circle and singing games:
"I'm going to wash that man right out of my hair", "Show your feet" etc., (see "Getting used to the water by playing games")

→ Simple dances:
Bingo, Macarena, Polonaise

→ Creating movements to music: movements can be invented according to the type of music and performed either individually or in a group.

Variations:
- moving to the music in the water individually
- moving to the music in the water in a group
- moving to the music in the water in a large group
- creating elements of artistic and synchronized swimming

III ELEMENTARY SWIMMING TECHNIQUES

"Life is short but a smile only takes a second."

(A Cuban Saying)

3 Preliminary Considerations, Teaching Techniques in Swimming Instruction

Before introducing methods for the choice of the first swimming technique, we will first briefly discuss some ideas on how to start teaching techniques for swimming, and what the various ways are that lead up to moving forward in water.

Learning a technique traditionally assumes that there is an "ideal technique". Usually these are depicted in diagrams, showing a technique being performed by a world champion, and which are presented as being the standard that should be reached as a norm. For example, the illustrated book series by Counsilman, showing swimming techniques, have been used as the standard work by generations of swimming instructors. Such a viewpoint on swimming techniques does not do justice to the variety of movements possible in, on and under water. The deciding factor is not the orientation on precisely-given norms when learning swimming techniques and moving in the water; rather, it is the individual contact with the element water and the resulting movements in it that count. "The most important thing is not learning an action (of part of a movement or a stereotype motor skill – to mention some other terms for the same thing) when teaching or learning motor skills in sport; rather, it is learning the relation between the action and the function as part of the required movement task." (Göhner, 1984: 33).

The task of schools and other institutions, such as swimming clubs, life-saving organizations etc., in teaching swimming should not, therefore, consist primarily of teaching a few standardized swimming techniques as quickly as possible. It is much more about placing more emphasis on the development of the whole personality. A broad training program that is not fixed on just one sport, but aims at coordination ability and a comprehensive training of the perception and the movements, should be aimed at. "The goal of every practice and training session consists not only of improving a sports technique or learning it in a coordinated fashion, but also of improving the individual motor skills." (Hirtz, 1994: 117).

In order to do justice to this method of looking at learning to swim, there needs to be a re-thinking – not only in dealing with beginner swimming instruction. It is necessary to move away from a one-sided learning of techniques towards a broader learning of the movements, which is orientated to the experiences, and which gives the pupils an opportunity to train their individual perception. The learning of a chosen swimming technique should also be orientated towards this way of thinking. " *The fundamental pillars of this kind of technique training are based on a broad and varied training, the training of the coordination ability and the training of cognitive perception.*" (Nagel & Wulkop, 1992: 27).

Many programs promoting sports, therefore, try increasingly to teach a wide range of movement skills that is as broad as possible. To make diverse experiences with movement possible, one should use games and exercises from different kinds of sport. This is why it is also recommended, when teaching a swimming technique, to promote creativity and attain the teaching of a diverse repertoire of movements. This can be achieved easier by setting movement tasks rather than by giving exact movement instructions. The coordination ability is also important as a basic for learning swimming techniques. "Well-developed coordination abilities are very important in teaching the motor system to assimilate motor actions and combinations of actions and skills" (Hirtz, 1994: 125).

The close relation between perception and action is emphasized by many authors, especially teachers of motor skills, and psychologists specializing in motor skills (Kiphard, Irmischer, Zimmer et al). "Movement is an action linking perception and the execution of that movement." (Loibl & Leist, 1990: 19). In the following, we will describe methods of learning first swimming techniques that agree with this interpretation. The focus is on a series of techniques that permit a variety of experiences with movement and that perception and movement are understood as being a linked process.

This means learning to move starts with simple movement exercises, which open up many opportunities for movements and which stimulate children's creativity. Making exercise tasks more specific can teach them how best to move in the water. Experiencing buoyancy and forward movement on an individual basis, can teach an intrinsic understanding of the movement which is greater than that of external movement exercises that children are required to carry out.

As the consideration of "optimal movement processes" is especially justified in competitive sports, it must be mentioned here as well. Therefore, in order to set an example, the traditional manner of teaching techniques will be presented in a methodical range of exercises.

The methodical way of learning a swimming technique is divided into the following 5 partial learning goals. After the basic motor experiences of swimming for beginners, leg movements (kicking) are introduced. The second partial learning goal is the arm stroke. When the arm stroke and kicking movements are mastered, the coordination of arms and legs can begin. Finally overall coordination can be learned by introducing breathing (rhythmical breathing appropriate to the particular swimming technique).

3.1   The Various Ways of Leg Action

Leg movements for the first independent forward movement in water can be introduced in different ways. As the possibilities of various movements are paramount in all areas of swimming for beginners – especially in the section on 'getting used to the water in a playful manner and on first movement experiences' – we will first present a method which is the most suitable for achieving these goals (cf., Chapters 2.1 and 2.7). The children can practice elementary leg movements using simple movement exercises that focus on their creativity, on experimenting with various sorts of movements and on their own experiences during the learning process.

Alternatively, precise movement instructions can introduce a technique (e.g. the crawl kick) by using various methodical exercises. This method is often emphasized in swimming instruction that is more 'teacher oriented'. Such a method of learning the crawl kick is presented in Chapter 3.1.2.

3.1.1 Movement Exercises with the Legs

Even as toddlers, or in swimming for babies, children can gain first movement experiences that lead to being able to do leg movements. Children can try out first paddling movements that lead to the leg kick movements later, while being held lying on their back. During passive gliding (being pulled while lying on the back or the stomach) the elements of the first alternating movement of the legs can be developed further. If the children are small or handicapped, and thus have little forward propulsion ability, these movements can be strengthened by using flippers so that the children soon become independent. An additional step towards independence and reducing the amount of help from a partner can be made by being pulled on a swimming bar or a swimming board. When a child is able to glide in the partner's wake, it doesn't take long to learn to swim on its own using elementary leg movements.

The following movement tasks lead to independent swimming with leg movements:

a) Leg movements made on the spot while lying on the back

Leg movements made while on the back and being held:
The partner holds the child, lying on its back in the water with its head resting on the partner's shoulders, close to the body. The partner can now lower his shoulders more deeply in the water so that first the child's head is carried by the shoulder, then by the shoulder and the water, and finally, just by the water.

In this position the child can be made to do the following elementary leg kicking exercises:

- Who can kick with the legs while lying on his back?
- Who can kick the most?
- Who can splash the most water while kicking?
- Who can splash the least water while kicking?

Elementary leg movements while sitting at the edge of the pool:
The child can be made to do the following exercises when sitting at the edge of the pool:

- Who can kick the most?
- Who can splash the most water while kicking?
- Who can splash the least water while kicking?
- Who can make the water boil?
- Who can kick with his legs stretched out?

Elementary leg movements while lying on the back in a press-up position at the steps:
Exercises: see above

b) Leg kicking movements lying on the back and moving forwards

Leg movements while the child is being held lying on its back:
When pulling a child on his back the child can actively assist the forward movement with "kicking movements" of the legs. These elementary movements can be initially assisted with flippers. The children quickly learn the first active swimming movements. Being pulled directly by a partner can be replaced by being pulled on a swimming bar or a swimming board.

Variations:
- with flippers and the help of a partner
- with a swimming bar and flippers
- with a swimming board and flippers
- with flippers
- without aids

Leg movements while the child is lying on its back and gliding in the partner's wake
Gliding in a partner's wake leads to being able to glide on one's own. Elementary leg kicking movements can increase the gliding distance. The following tasks lead to a kicking action which moves the swimmer forward:
- Who can kick while lying on his back and glide for a longer distance on his own?
- Who can kick a lot while gliding?
- Who can move the legs calmly while gliding so he only splashes a little water?
- Who can kick with his legs stretched out?

Variations: see above

Leg movements while the child is gliding on its own on its back:
After pulling the child along lying on its back and gliding in a partner's wake, gliding on its own can be practiced as a next stage. This can be extended by using elementary leg kicking movements. The exercises can be set in a similar way as explained above.

Variations:
- with flippers and the help of a partner
- with a swimming bar and flippers
- with a swimming board and flippers
- with flippers
- without aids

c) Leg movements whilst the child is lying on its front:

After doing elementary leg kicking movements on the spot and being pulled along on the stomach, the child can try out different leg movements also in a stomach prone position, which can be modified gradually until they become more and more effective. For tasks and variations: see above (Sections a) and b)).

3.1.2   Series of Movements Used in the Crawl

a) Structure of the methodical group of exercises:

A methodical group of exercises introduces a sport technique in a systematic fashion. Of the different versions of teaching pupils sport techniques, the following structure of a methodical group of exercises has proven itself:

- *Systematic warm-up:* running, hopping, jumping, etc., intensive movement forwards. Or for swimming: warm-up swimming.
- *Warming-up games:* e.g. Running and catching games, little ball-games
- Gymnastics or stretching

Particular exercises for warming up

- Special gymnastics exercises
- Exercises leading to the techniques being introduced

Introducing a Movement Technique
There are a number of different methods which can be used to introduce a movement technique:

- Visual methods:
  - demonstrate or let someone demonstrate
  - pictures, illustrated strips, posters or charts, films, videos
- Acoustic methods:
  - description of the movement
  - explanations of the movement
- Kinaesthetic methods:
  - demonstrating the movement

Development of exercises
First of all, the new technique is carried out as an easy exercise. The easiness of the exercise can gradually be reduced, until the final exercise is carried out.

Application of the learned technique in games and exercises
The technique learned can now be applied to very different exercises or to simple games.

b) Methodical series of exercises for the crawl kick

General preparatory training in the form of games or warm-up exercises may be followed by specific preparation exercises, e.g., those aimed at improving the suppleness of the feet and the hip joints. The movement can be either described or demonstrated using visual methods (see above).

The **description of the movement** should include the most important criteria of the crawl kick:

The crawl kick is an **alternating** leg kicking movement, where the **impulse for movement comes from the hips. The legs and feet are stretched but relaxed,** while the feet are **turned** slightly **inwards.** We distinguish between the instep kick (downward kick in the front position) and the sole kick. **During the instep kick, the leg is bent passively by the water pressure.** The thigh introduces the movement followed by the kicking of the lower leg and the feet. This is also called the flipper effect. **During the sole kick, the**

leg is virtually stretched. For a dynamic leg kicking movement you need a **quick change from the instep to the sole kick.** Here **both legs kick at the same time** (with the same intensity) crossing past each other as they do the movement. The **amplitude of the kick** should be 60-70 cm for adult swimmers. A good flat position in the water is ensured by resting the head on the water.

Developing the exercise for the crawl kick:
Exercises should allow this technique to be practiced initially as simply as possible. Because the crawl kick is easier to do when lying on the back, most of the initial exercises should be carried out in this position. When the crawl kick on the back has been more or less mastered, it can be introduced step by step lying on the stomach. The advantage of this parallel development of the front and backstroke crawl kick is that the swimmer feels confident in either position and is able to move in both.

→ Kicking with one leg while standing
The child stands sideways on to the edge of the pool, so that he is able to swing the other backwards and forwards in the water. Another child can assist the first child to keep his balance by holding on to him. The first child swings the leg backwards and forwards while paying special attention to the position of the feet. The feet should be stretched out and turned inwards.

Goals and points to watch out for
In this exercise the stretching out and inwards turning position of the feet should be particularly practiced. **If the exercise (correct foot positioning) is not performed correctly it is recommended that it be corrected at this point.**

Variations: • kicking with one leg while standing at the pool steps
              • kicking first with one leg while standing and then with the other

→ Leg kicking movement while sitting at the edge of the pool
The children sit on the edge of the pool with their legs in the water and perform the crawl kick with their legs as explained above. In order to ensure that the kick movement is not done from their knees, the children should sit with their bottoms close to the edge of the pool supporting themselves with their hands placed as far away behind them as possible.

Goals and points to watch out for
The impulse of the kick comes from the hips, while the legs are "stretched but relaxed". If this exercise is not performed correctly (cyclic movements, legs not stretched out), it is recommended that it be corrected at this point.

Variation:
- who can splash the most water when kicking?
- who can splash the least water when kicking?
- who can make the water boil?
- who can kick with stretched legs?

→ Leg kicking movement while lying on the back in a press-up position at the steps
All the children lie on their backs in a back press-up position at the steps and practice the crawl kick. This exercise can also be done in pairs, with the partner always taking the role of an observer.

Goals and points to watch out for
Regular and rhythmical kicking.
- The position of the body in the water should be flat so that the impulse comes from the hip. To make this possible the partner has to take the head back with the shoulders in the water.
- Medium sized amplitude of movement

→ Leg kicking movement while gliding passively lying on the back
One partner pulls the other who is lying on his back, close to the body. The partner being pulled does the crawl kick.

Goals and points to watch out for
Criteria of the crawl kick that have been practiced up to now (see above)

Variation:
- one partner pulls the other along on his back by holding him under the armpits close to his body. The partner being pulled does the crawl kick with flippers
- one partner pulls the other along on his back by holding him under the armpits with his arms stretched out. The partner being pulled does the crawl kick
- one partner holds the other under the armpits and pulls him along on his back with his arms stretched out. The partner who is being pulled does the crawl kick with flippers

- one partner pulls the other along on his back with a swimming bar and flippers
- one partner pulls the other along on his back using a swimming board and flippers
- one partner pulls the other along on his back with flippers
- one partner pulls the other along on his back without aids

→ Leg kicking movement, reducing the amount of the partner's help
Grasping him under the armpits, one partner pulls the other on his back and lets him glide a short distance in his wake. The partner being pulled does the crawl kick in order to increase the gliding distance.

Variations: • see above (leg kicking movement while gliding passively lying on the back)

→ Leg kicking movement while actively gliding
After pushing themselves off the wall of the pool, the children come into the gliding position and then go half a length of the learner's pool by using only the crawl leg kick.

Variations: • using the crawl kick and a swimming bar and flippers gliding on the back
- using the crawl kick with a swimming board and flippers gliding on the back
- using only the crawl kick and flippers to glide half a length of the pool
- using only the crawl kick and flippers to glide a whole length of the pool
- using only the crawl kick to glide a whole length of the pool, this time without flippers

→ Repetitive exercising over short distances
Initially the pupils swim short distances (the width of the pool) repeatedly in order to practice the crawl kick and to consolidate the movement process. Any mistakes can be corrected during these exercises.

→ Increasing the distance

When the pupils have almost perfected the movements of the crawl kick, the swimming distance can be increased.

Variations:
- a width of the pool twice
- a width of the pool three or more times
- a full length of the pool
- several lengths of the pool

→ Increasing the intensity

When the crawl kick has been consolidated by practicing it repetitively and swimming longer distances, the intensity can be also increased, e.g., by a swimming competition across the width of the pool.

Variations:
- who can do a width of the pool the fastest?
- swimming the width of the pool twice
- swimming a full length of the pool fast

Use in games and exercises

When leg movements can be carried out almost without any mistakes, even over longer distances, competitive games and exercises can be carried out:
- Doing leg kicking movements against resistance:
  The swimming board is held crossways to the direction in which the pupils wants to move. The pupil now does the crawl kick pushing against the increased resistance.
- Ousting the partner:
  Two swimmers hold one swimming board in the middle of the pool standing facing each other. Each of them then tries to force the other to the other side with the crawl kick.
- Relay games:
  A turning-around relay, tag relay, relays carrying objects etc.

→ Crawl kick while lying on the stomach

In the previous chapter the crawl kick was introduced with elementary exercises being done parallel lying on the back or on the stomach. It was then developed further, first of all while lying on the back for methodical reasons. The games and exercises of the group of exercises already presented can be easily used now for performing the kick when lying on the stomach.

Games and exercises as explained above

3.2   Moving the Arms

Similarly to leg strokes, arm strokes can be developed based on the experiences gained in doing elementary movements (cf., Chapters 2.7 and 3.1). Passive gliding (with a partner pulling) can lead to the first elementary swimming movements and can be worked on by adding the arm stroke lying on the back or the stomach.

Here we will show how the pupils can experience these movements in performing various simple movement exercises walking in the water. By modifying the exercises they can be developed further into achieving forward movement. All these movements form the basis for the further development of swimming techniques, from which, for example, the technique of the crawl arm stroke can be brought out. The following movement exercises give step-by-step training in the crawl arm stroke by getting the pupils to walk around in the pool (the inductive teaching progress):

Walking with and without using the arms
The exercise "Who can walk through the water on his own?" makes the children try out different types of movements (forwards, backwards or sideways, with and without using the arms and other variations).

Goal: The children find out that they can walk more quickly when using their arms than when not using their arms.
Task: Who can walk through the water on his own?
Variations: • who is the quickest?
                 • races using the arms and not using the arms
                 • relay races
                 • walking forwards, backwards and sideways
                 • hopping, jumping, and running and hopping at the same time
                 • who can hop to the other side with the fewest jumps?

Walking using different arm strokes
As walking is quicker when using the arms, the children can now try out what other various ways there are to generate better forward movement while walking and using their arms.

Goal: The children find out that they are quicker when using the arms alternately than when using both arms simultaneously.

Exercise:	Who can walk through the water using different arm strokes?
Variations:	• who is the quickest?
	• races using both arms alternately and simultaneously
	• relay races
	• walking backwards and forwards

Walking with alternating arm strokes

As walking while using the alternating arm stroke is quicker, the children can now try out what various possibilities there are to permit better forward movement while walking and using their arms alternately.

Goal:	The children find out that they are quicker when using a long alternating arm stroke and that the forward movement should be executed with both arms steadily.
Exercise:	Who can walk through the water with alternating arm strokes?
Variations:	• short and longer alternating arm strokes.
	• both arms cause forward movement.
	• walking backwards and forwards.
Games:	• The children walk through the water in groups, moving their arms to the same rhythm as far as possible.
	• Eights: Eight children walk behind each other, moving their arms to the same rhythm as far as possible.
	• Races with alternating use of the arms.
	• Relay races

The positions of the hand during the arm stroke

The children can now try out different positions with their hands and find out which position permits which forward movement.

Goal:	The children find out that the stretched and slightly opened or closed hand improves forward movement.
Task:	Who can walk through the water while using the arms with different positions of the hands?
Variations:	• trying out extreme positions of the hands (fist, hand chopping the water, and others).
	• pulling the stretched and slightly opened or closed hand through the water.

- walking backwards and forwards.
- races using the arms and hands differently
- relay races

Long arm strokes while walking

As long arm strokes permit a longer forward movement, the children should, by carrying out suitable tasks, find out how they permit the longest possible forward movement by using their arms.

Goal: The children discover that walking with the upper body bowed makes a longer arm stroke possible.

Task: Who can walk through the water while using arm strokes of different lengths?

Variations: • walking through the water with short or long arm strokes
             • resting the upper body on the water and using the arms while walking.
             • walking backwards and forwards.
             • races while using the arms differently
             • relay races

Immersing the hands

The children walk through the water and are told to watch and   discover how and where to best immerse their hands into the water in order to introduce a long arm stroke.

Goal: The children find out that the hand can be best immersed when the fingertips are immersed first while the elbow stays up. The place where the hands immerse should be in front of the shoulder (the right hand in front of the right shoulder).

Task: Who can walk through the water while using arm strokes and at the same time note how the hands are immersed?

Variations: • see above

Different Patterns of Hand Movement

Since long arm strokes improve forward movement, the children should find out by means of suitable exercises how they can best move forward in the water with the use of their arms. The task can work out the difference between the straight and the S-shaped arm stroke.

Goal:	The children find out that the S-shaped arm stroke permits a longer forward arm movement.
Task:	Who can walk through the water and best achieve a forward movement by using the arms?
Variations:	• walking through the water using short or long arm strokes
	• walking through the water using straight and S-shaped arm strokes
	• walking backwards and forwards
	• races using the arms differently
	• relay races

Swinging phase in the arm stroke

When walking through the water by using the arms, the children should note how the arms are swung forwards best in the swinging phase.

Goal:	The children find out that the arm swings forwards best by holding the elbow up high close to the longitudinal axis of the body.
Exercise:	Who can walk through the water using arm strokes and at the same time note the swinging phase?
Variations:	• see above

Position in the water during an arm stroke

When the children move forward in the water using alternating arm movements and resting their upper body down on the water, they can remove their legs from the bottom of the pool briefly in order to swim a short distance unassisted. The children can become aware of this "swimming experience" themselves or by watching other children. So that swimming unassisted over longer distances can also be achieved, the position in the water must be improved. Using appropriate exercises the children can find this out by themselves.

Goal:	Taking the legs off the bottom and improving the position of the body in the water.
Exercise:	Who can rest the upper body forwards on the water and move forwards by using the arms alternately?
Variations:	• see above

Arm stroke with the help of a partner

Goal: Optimizing the position in the water and the crawl arm stroke.

Crawl arm stroke while being pushed along
A partner lies on the Water and the other pushes him by holding his hips. The partner who is being pushed executes the crawl arm stroke.

Variations:
- slow and controlled arm stroke
- rolling with the shoulders facilitates the forward swinging of the arm in the swinging phase and the pressure phase of the arm under the body

Reducing the amount of help from the partner

Goal: Optimizing the position in the water and swimming without assistance using the crawl arm stroke

Reducing the amount of help from the partner in steps
A partner lies on the water, the other pushes him, while the partner who is being pushed executes the crawl arm stroke. Just before reaching the edge of the pool the partner lets go
so that the learner now swims a short distance without any assistance.

Variations:
- increasing the distance that is swum without assistance
- the pushed partner also puts a pull-buoy between his thighs
- the partner is pushed a short distance only, before he swims on without assistance with the pull-buoy

Gliding with a pull-buoy using the crawl arm stroke
The children put pull-buoys between their thighs and swim across the width of the pool using the crawl arm stroke.

Variations:
- gradually increasing the distance that is swum without assistance
- swimming across the width of the swimming pool
- swimming a number of times across the width of the swimming pool (in deep water).

Criteria for the crawl arm stroke

Before the crawl arm stroke is consolidated and trained using additional games and exercises, the criteria of the movement process that have already been practiced, can be summarized as follows:

The crawl arm stroke is an **alternating arm stroke**. The arms are used alternately and **regularly** while moving forwards. You can distinguish between a swinging phase, and a stroke and pressure phase as an underwater phase. During the **swinging phase** the arm is swung forwards with the **elbow raised up close to the longitudinal axis of the body**. With fingertips first, the hand is immersed **in front of the shoulder**. When the **stroke phase** begins, the arm is turned inwards (inward rotation, a pronation movement) and stretched forwards and downwards in order to press against the water. The hand is then pulled down in a slight outwards curve and the **arm is increasingly bent** until it has reached the maximal bend of about 90° at the height of the shoulders. The **S-shaped** stroke is continued during the pressure phase, **until** the arm stroke is finished at the **thigh**. The arm is then swung again forward. During the stroke and pressure phase **the body rolls** at the shoulders around the longitudinal axis of the body.

Repetitive exercises over short distances

To practice the crawl arm stroke and consolidate the movement process, the pupils first repeatedly swim short distances (widths of the pool), during which any mistakes can be corrected.

Crawl Arm Stroke and Increasing the Distance

When the movements of the crawl arm stroke can be performed virtually fault-free, the swimming distance can be increased:

Variations:
- doing a width of the pool twice
- doing a width of the pool three or more times
- doing a full length of the pool
- swimming a full length of the pool several times

Increasing intensity

When the crawl arm stroke has been learned properly, the intensity can be increased, e.g., in swimming races across the width of the pool.

Application in games and exercises

See above (crawl kick).

3.3 Overall Coordination (Without Breathing)

The process leading to overall coordination without breathing is only briefly described here. When the leg kick and the arm stroke of the crawl have more or less been mastered, the following methodical steps can lead to overall coordination:

→ Swimming with the crawl arm stroke across the width of the pool, the legs are passive.

→ Swimming with the crawl arm stroke across the width of the pool, the legs swing loosely.

→ Swimming with the crawl arm stroke across the width of the pool, the leg kick is deliberate.

→ Swimming with the crawl arm stroke across the width of the pool, the kicking of the legs is deliberately increased.

→ Swimming with the crawl leg stroke across the width of the pool. From the middle of the pool onwards the arms are added to the leg movement.

→ After pushing off from the edge of the wall the legs immediately begin to kick and the arms are added directly after surfacing.

Variations: • doing a width of the pool twice
• doing a width of the pool three or more times
• a full length of the pool
• several full lengths of the pool
• with flippers

3.4 Breathing

As the introduction to breathing in the section on Swimming for Beginners has been described in detail, here is a brief overview of the individual methodical steps.

→ Breathing out into the water

→ Making the breathing rhythmical

→ Breathing technique best suited to the first swimming technique

During the crawl you breathe to the side.

Breaststroke: When breathing in, the head is lifted (with or without the help of a partner) – see the section on *Breathing* (Chapter 2.3)

3.5 Overall Coordination and Breathing

Rhythmical breathing

Rhythmical breathing suitable for the crawl technique:

→ **Lying on the stomach in a press-up position at the steps**: breathing out slowly into the water and turning the head to one side briefly when breathing in.

Variation: • turn the head to the other side as well

→ Rhythmical breathing while moving forward:
  • Walking through the water
  • Passive gliding (being pulled by the partner)
  • While gliding with a swimming board

Coordinating breathing and leg movement

The rhythmical breathing is now coordinated with the crawl kick:

→ **Passive gliding (being pulled by the partner):**
  The partner being pulled performs the crawl kick, breathing regularly to one side. His partner pulls him with his arms stretched forwards. This enables him to actively support the turning movement to the side while his partner is breathing.

→ While gliding with a swimming board

→ While gliding with the crawl leg kick

Coordinating breathing and the arm stroke

First of all, breathing and arm strokes are coordinated so breathing is carried out on one side only using only one arm for the arm stroke. The breathing is then coordinated with the alternating arm stroke.

Alternating arm stroke and breathing while standing:

Standing at the edge of the pool with the upper body bent forward, one arm holds the overflow gutter and the other performs the arm stroke movement.

At the same time the pupil breathes out slowly into the water and turns his head to one side quickly while breathing in.

Alternating arm stroke and breathing while moving forwards:
→ Crouching down and walking through the water, adding breathing to the arm stroke

→ One partner pulls the other through the water with a stretched arm, the partner who is being pulled breathes in quickly to one side and breathes out slowly into the water. The pulling partner can actively support the turning movement to the side by turning the partner to one side by the arm.

Photo 12: *One-sided arm stroke and breathing while being pulled*

→ Gliding with a swimming board: One arm performs the crawl arm stroke, coordinating it with breathing.

→ Going from gliding to alternating arm strokes and adding breathing.

Variations: • breathing out to the other side as well
• breathing in time to a 3-beat rhythm
• other breathing rhythms: 4-beat, 5-beat.

Breathing and overall coordination

One partner pulls the other. The partner being pulled breathes quickly to one side and adds the kick to the one-sided arm stroke.

Being pulled by the arms alternately out of gliding and adding breathing and kicking.

Variations: • see above

4   Index

5   Photo and Illustration Credits

Photos 1-4, 6-12	Carsten Henrichsmeier
Figures 7-12	Uwe Rheker
Figures 13-26	Michael Blase, Helmut Böhmer
Figures 27-38	Michael Blase, Helmut Böhmer, Uwe Rheker
Figures 39-45	Michael Blase
Logo	Artemis Herber
Coverphotos:	Michael von Fisenne
Coverdesign:	Birgit Engelen

6 Literature

Ahr, B.: Schwimmen mit Babys und Kleinkindern. Stuttgart 1989.

Arenhoevel, D., Deissler, A. & Vögtle, A.: Die Bibel. Freiburg 1965 (15. Aufl.).

Bauermeister, H.: In der Badewanne fängt es an. München 1972.

Becker, K.-P.: Full Participation and Equality. In: Blickensrorfer, J., Dohrenbusch, H. & Klein, F. (Hrsg.): Ethik in der Sonderpädagogik. Berlin 1988, 10-19.

Beigel-Guhl, K. & Brinckmann, A.: Wassergymnastik. Hamburg 1989.

Blücher, V. G.: Jugend, Bildung und Freizeit (Hrsg. vom Jugendwerk der Deutschen Shell). Hamburg/Bielefeld 1966.

Bracken, H. v.: Vorurteile gegen behinderte Kinder, ihre Familien und Schulen. Berlin 1981 (2. Aufl.).

Bresges, L.: Schwimmen im ersten und zweiten Lebensjahr. München 1973.

Brettschneider, W.-D. & Bräutigam, M.: Sport in der Alltagswelt von Jugendlichen. Forschungsbericht (Hrsg: Kultusministerium NRW). Düsseldorf 1990.

Brettschneider, W.-D. & Rheker, U.: Bewegung, Spiel und Sport mit behinderten Kindern und Jugendlichen. (Hrsg: Ministerium für Stadtentwicklung, Kultur und Sport des Landes NRW). Heft 45 der Reihe: „Materialien zum Sport in Nordrhein-Westfalen". Düsseldorf 1996.

Brettschneider, W.-D. & Brandl-Bredenbeck, H. P.: Sportkultur und jugendliches Selbstkonzept. Eine interkulturell vergleichende Studie über Deutschland und die USA. Weinheim/München 1997.

Buntrock, M.: Meer. Spezielle Musik zum Entspannen, zum Lernen und für Mentales Training. Essen.

Cloerkes, G.: Einstellung und Verhalten gegenüber Körperbehinderten. Eine kritische Bestandsaufnahme der Ergebnisse internationaler Forschung. Berlin 1985 (3. Aufl.).

Counsilman, J. E.: Schwimmen. Frankfurt a. M. 1971.

Counsilman, J. E.: Handbuch des Sport-Schwimmens. Bockenem 1980.

Csikszentmihalyi, M.: Das Flow-Erlebnis: Jenseits von Angst und Langeweile: im Tun aufgehen. Stuttgart 1996.

Cube, F. v.: Gefährliche Sicherheit. München 1990.

Daniel, K.: Der Einfluß der Wechselzugschwimmarten als erstgelernte Schwimmtechnik auf Motivation und Lernerfolge im Schwimmunterricht. In: Kölner Beiträge zur Sportwissenschaft Band 2. Köln 1973.

Deci, E. L. & Ryan, M.: Intrinsic Motivation and Selfdetermination in Human Behaviour. New York 1985.

Diederley, H.: Schwimmen mit geistig behinderten Kindern und Jugendlichen. Rheinstetten 1975.

Diem, L., Bürgerer, R., Bussmann, U., Groten, H. & Siegling, V.: Säuglingsschwimmen. Braunschweig 1981.

Dordel, S.: Bewegungsförderung in der Schule. Handbuch des Schulsonderturnens/Sportförderunterricht. Dortmund 1993 (3. Aufl.).

Durlach, F.-J.: Spielen, Bewegen, Schwimmen. Schorndorf 1994.

Durlach, F.-J.: Erlebniswelt Wasser. Spielen, Gestalten, Schwimmen. Schorndorf 1998 (2. Aufl.).

Eberwein, H. (Hrsg.): Behinderte und Nichtbehinderte lernen gemeinsam. Handbuch der Integrationspädagogik. Weinheim/Basel 1994.

Fediuk, F.: Einführung in den Integrationssport. Teil 1: Pädagogisch-konzeptionelle Grundlagen. Kassel 1992.

Feldkamp, M. & Danielciek, I.: Krankengymnastische Behandlung der zerebralen Bewegungsstörung im Kindesalter. München 1976 (2. Aufl.).

Fonance, J.: Babys lernen schwimmen. Niedernhausen/Ts. 1980.

Frank, G.: Koordinative Fähigkeiten im Schwimmen: Der Schlüssel zur perfekten Technik. Schorndorf 1996.

Gabler, H.: Zum Problem der Angst beim Anfängerschwimmen. In: Volck, G. (Hrsg.): Schwimmen in der Schule, Schorndorf 1977, 121-128.

Gaulhofer, K. & Streicher, M.: Grundzüge des österreichischen Schulturnens. Wien 1922.

Gaulhofer, K. & Streicher, M.: Das neue Schulturnen. Weinheim 1962.

Gildenhard, N.: Vielseitiger Schwimmunterricht in der Vorschule und Eingangsstufe. Schorndorf 1977.

Gill, J. K.: Möglichkeiten des Sports bei der Rehabilitation Körperbehinderter. Rheinstetten 1975.

Göhner, U.: Anforderungen an die Gestaltung von funktional angemessenem Tennisunterricht. In: Kähler, R. (Red.): Bewegungswahrnehmung und Bewegungsvermittlung im Tennis. DVS-Protokolle, Heft 13/14, Clausthal-Zellerfeld 1984, 32-50.

Graumann, D., Lohmann, H. & Pflesser; W.: Schwimmen in Schule und Verein. Celle 1992 (5. Aufl.).

Hasler-Rietmann, B.: Therapeutische Aspekte sportlicher Betätigungen: Schwimmen mit zerebral bewegungsgestörten Kindern. In: Feldkamp, M. & Danielciek, I.: Krankengymnastische Behandlung der zerebralen Bewegungsstörung im Kindesalter. München 1976, 2. Aufl., 264-278.

Hellmich, H.: Schwimmen im dritten und vierten Lebensjahr. München 1974.

Hetz, G.: Lehrgang mit Flossen. In: Wilke, K.: Anfängerschwimmen. Reinbek bei Hamburg 1979.

Hildebrandt, R.: „Schwimmen lernen" als Erschließung des Bewegungsraumes Wasser. In: Sportunterricht, Schorndorf, 42 (1993), 5, 199-204.

Hirtz, P.: Motorische Handlungskompetenz als Funktion motorischer Fähigkeiten. In: Hirtz, P., Kirchner, G. & Pöhlmann, R. (Hrsg.): Sportmotorik. Grundlagen, Anwendungen und Grenzgebiete. Kassel 1994, 117-147.

Hirtz, P., Kirchner, G. & Pöhlmann, R. (Hrsg.): Sportmotorik. Grundlagen, Anwendungen und Grenzgebiete. Kassel 1994.

Hoffsümmer, W.: Kurzgeschichten 1. 255 Kurzgeschichten für Gottesdienst, Schule und Gruppe. Mainz 1992a (13. Aufl.).

Hoffsümmer, W.: Kurzgeschichten 2. 222 Kurzgeschichten für Gottesdienst, Schule und Gruppe. Mainz 1992b (8. Aufl.).

Innenmoser, J.: Schwimmspaß für Behinderte. Bockenem 1988 (2. Aufl.).

Innenmoser, J.: Gliedmaßenschäden. In: Bundesminister für Arbeit und Sozialordnung (Hrsg.): Forschungsbericht „Bewegung, Spiel und Sport mit Behinderten und von Behinderung Bedrohten. Indikationskatalog und Methodenmanual" Bd. 1-3. Bonn 1990.

Irmischer, T.: Motopädagogik bei geistig Behinderten. Schorndorf 1980.

Jacobo, P.: Damit unser Leben gelingen kann: Erzählungen und Märchen, aufgeschlossen für Gespräch in Schule, Gemeinde und Jugendarbeit. Mainz 1981

Jansen, G. W.: Die Einstellung der Gesellschaft zu Körperbehinderten. Rheinstetten 1981, 4. Aufl.

Joeres, U.: Schwimmen. Unterrichtsmaterialien zur Sportlehrerausbildung für den schulischen und außerschulischen Bereich. Schorndorf 1979.

John, H. & Johnen, H.: Alternatives Schwimmen. Aachen 1983.

Kanter, G. O.: Gemeinsame Unterrichtung. Behinderte und nichtbehinderte Kinder und Jugendliche in einer sich verändernden Welt. In: Geistige Behinderung 36 (1988), 1-3.

Kiphard, E. J.: Motopädagogik. Dortmund 1979.

Kobi, E.: Was bedeutet Integration? Analyse eines Begriffs. In: Eberwein, H. (Hrsg.): Behinderte und Nichtbehinderte lernen gemeinsam. Handbuch der Integrationspädagogik. Weinheim/Basel 1994, 71-79.

Kosel, H.: Behindertensport: Körper- und Sinnesbehinderte; Handbuch für Sportlehrer, Übungsleiter, Ärzte, Krankengymnasten, Erzieher und Studierende. München 1981.

Kultusministerium des Landes Nordrhein-Westfahlen: Weiterentwicklung der sonderpädagogischen Förderung in Schulen. Düsseldorf 1995.

Kurz, D.: Elemente des Schulsports: Grundlagen einer pragmatischen Fachdidaktik. Schorndorf 1990.

Kurz, D. & Volck, G.: Zur didaktischen Begründung des Schwimmens in der Schule. In: Volck, G. (Hrsg.): Schwimmen in der Schule. Schorndorf 1977, 41-58.

Landesinstitut für Schule und Weiterbildung; NRW (Hrsg.): Mehr Sicherheit im Schulsport. Teil IV: Ergänzungshandreichung Sportbereich Schwimmen. Bielefeld 1993.

Lange, J.: Schwimmen – Teil des Handlungsfeldes Sport. In: Volck, G. (Hrsg.): Schwimmen in der Schule. Schorndorf 1977, 9-40.

Lause, R.: Geistig Behinderte erlernen das Schwimmen. Dortmund 1992.

Levenger, C.: Baby-Schwimmen – spielend im Wasser lernen. München 1988.

Lewin; G.: Schwimmsport. Berlin 1970.

Lewin, G.: Schwimmen mit kleinen Leuten. Berlin 1975.

Lewin, G.: Schwimmen kinderleicht, Frankfurt/Berlin 1994.

Loibl, J. & Leist, K.-H.: Vom gefühlvollen Sich-Bewegen und seiner Vermittlung. In: Sportpädagogik 14 (1990), 4, 19-25.

Loibl, J.: Im Lehren und lernen – Räume erschließen. In: Sportpädagogik 16 (1992), 4, 28-31.

Lorenzen, H.: Lehrbuch des Versehrtensports. Stuttgart 1961.

Lorenzen, H.: Behinderte schwimmen. Zur Biomechanik des Schwimmens mit körperlichen, geistigen und seelischen Schäden. Wuppertal 1970.

Mehl, E.: Antike Schwimmkunst. München 1927.

Mehl, E.: Ein Blick in die Weltgeschichte des Schwimmens. In: Joeres. U.: Schwimmen: Unterrichtsmaterialien zur Sportlehrerausbildung für den schulischen und außerschulischen Bereich. Schorndorf 1979, 21-22.

Minsel, M.: Zur Methodik des Anfängerschwimmens: ein erziehungs-psychologischer Versuch mit 120 körperlich gesunden und 60 körperbehinderten Kindern im Grundschulalter. Ahrensburg bei Hamburg 1974.

Nagel, V. & Wulkop, M.: Techniktraining im Hockey. Hamburg 1992.

Neumann, V.-H.: So lernen kleine Kinder Schwimmen. München 1969.

Oerter, R. & Montada, L.: Entwicklunspsychologie. München/Weinheim 1987.

Ott, D. & Schmidt, N.: Aquagymnastik. Körper- und Bewegungstraining im Wasser. Aachen 1995.

Pahncke, W.: Schwimmen in Vergangenheit und Gegenwart. Band 1 Geschichte des Schwimmsports in Deutschland von den Anfängen bis 1945. Berlin 1979.

Rheker, U.: Familien-Freizeitgruppe mit behinderten und nichtbehinderten Kindern. In: Bös, K., Doll-Tepper, G. & Trosien, G. (Hrsg.): Geistig Behinderte in Bewegung, Spiel und Sport. Marburg 1989, 123-146.

Rheker, U.: Sport für alle – auch für und mit behinderten Menschen? In: Motorik 16 (1993), 130-138.

Rheker, U.: Spiel und Sport für alle – Integrationssport für Familie, Verein und Freizeit. Aachen 1995 (2. Aufl.).

Rheker, U.: Bewegung, Spiel und Sport mit behinderten Kindern und Jugendlichen. (Hrsg.): Ministerium für Stadtentwicklung, Kultur und Sport des Landes NRW. Heft 45 der Reihe: „Materialien zum Sport in Nordrhein-Westfalen", Düsseldorf 1996a.

Rheker, U.: Integrationssport – Sport ohne Aussonderung. Darstellung eines praxisorientierten Ansatzes einer differenzierten Integrationspädagogik für den Sport von Menschen mit unterschiedlichen Voraussetzungen. Hamburg 1996b.

Rheker, U.: Integrationssport – Sport ohne Aussonderung. Darstellung eines praxisorientierten Ansatzes einer differenzierten Integrationspädagogik für den Sport von Menschen mit unterschiedlichen Voraussetzungen. Teil 2 Die Untersuchung (Microfiche). Paderborn 1996c.

Rheker, U.: Rollstuhlsport als spezielle Form des Integrationssports in Verein und Schule. In: Sportunterricht 46 (1997), 9, 395-404a.

Rheker, U.: „Tauchen mit behinderten Menschen". 1. internationales Symposion". Paderborn 1997b.

Rheker, U.: Integration through Games and Sport. Aachen, 2000.

Rheker, H.: Sport als Therapie. Berlin/München/Frankfurt 1971.

Sack, H.-G.: Soziale Funktion des Sportvereins im Jugendalter. Abschußbericht des gleichnamigen Projekts der Deutschen Sportjugend. Bd. 1. Frankfurt a. M. 1985.

Scheid, V.: Chancen der Integration durch Sport. Aachen 1995.

Scherler; K.-H.: Sensomotorische Entwicklung und materiale Erfahrung. Schorndorf 1975.

Scherler; K.-H.: Schwimmen. In: Sportpädagogik 5 (1981) 2, 14-21.

Schoot, P. v. d.: Aktivierungstheoretische Perspektiven als wissenschaftliche Grundlegung für den Sportunterricht mit geistig retardierten Kindern. Schorndorf 1976.

Schoot, P. v. d.: Indikationsrelevante Aussagen zu „Bewegung, Spiel und Sport mit Behinderten und von Behinderung Bedrohten". In: Bundesminister für Arbeit und Sozialordnung (Hrsg.): Forschungsbericht „Bewegung, Spiel und Sport mit Behinderten und von Behinderung Bedrohten. Indikationskatalog und Methodenmanual" Bd. 1-3. Bonn 1990, 3-97.

Schuchardt, E.: Ende der UNO-Dekade – Wende zur Integrationspädagogik/Andragogik. In: Eberwein, H. (Hrsg.): Behinderte und Nichtbehinderte lernen gemeinsam. Handbuch der Integrationspädagogik. Weinheim/Basel 1994, 202-214.

Silbereisen, R.: Entwicklungspsychologie: ein Handbuch in Schlüsselbegriffen. München 1983.

Silbereisen, R. & Kastner, P.: Jugend und Problemverhalten. Entwicklungspsychologische Perspektiven. In: Oerter, R. & Montada, L.: Entwicklunspsychologie. München/Weinheim 1987, 882-919.

Silvia, G.: Lehrgang mit dem Schwimmei. In: WILKE, K.: Anfängerschwimmen. Reinbek bei Hamburg 1979.

Speck, O.: Menschen mit geistiger Behinderung und ihre Erziehung. Ein heilpädagogisches Lehrbuch. München/Basel 1990.

Speck, O.: System Heilpädagogik. Eine ökologisch-reflexive Grundlegung. München/Basel 1991.

Volck, G. (Hrsg.): Schwimmen in der Schule. Schorndorf 1982 (2. Aufl.).

Weber-Witt, H.: Erlebnis Wasser. Therapeutische Übungen und Schwimmen. Berlin/Heidelberg/New York 1993.

Weizsäcker, R. v.: Behindertengerecht ist menschengerecht. In: ASbH-Brief 1993, 22-24.

Wiesner, K.: Natürlicher Schwimmunterricht. Wien 1925.

Wilke, K.: Anfängerschwimmen. Eine Dokumentationsstudie. Schorndorf 1976.

Wilke, K.: Anfängerschwimmen. Reinbek bei Hamburg 1979, 1992.

Wilke, K. (Hrsg.): Schwimmsport Praxis. Reinbek bei Hamburg 1988.

Wilke, K. & Daniel, K.: Schwimmen. Lernen, Üben, Trainieren. Wiesbaden 1996.

Zeitvogel, M.: Aquatraining. Reinbek bei Hamburg 1992.

Zielke, G.: Einsatz von Sonderpädagoginnen und Sonderpädagogen in integrativ arbeitenden Grundschulen. In: Eberwein, H. (Hrsg.): Behinderte und Nichtbehinderte lernen gemeinsam. Handbuch der Integrationspädagogik. Weinheim/Basel 1994, 277-284.

Zimmer, R. u. a.: Bewegung, Spiel und Sport mit Kindern. Aachen 1990.

Zimmer, R. & Cicurs, H.: Psychomotorik. Schorndorf 1987.

"Aquafun - First Steps" is the first in a series of three books:

Vol. 2:   Games and Fun for the Advanced, Spring 2005
Vol. 3:   Playing and Training Creatively for the Sport of Swimming, Spring 2006

1. Volume 2 "Games and Fun for the Advanced"

Volume 2 "Games and Fun for the Advanced" is devoted to the extensive variety of possibilities to have fun in the water after you have learned to swim.   The main emphasis is placed on adapting the proper games with a ball in water (water polo, water basketball, water volleyball, water football and underwater polo amongst others). Besides these, new games with the ball in water are introduced, such as water biathlon, aqua baseball etc. The large sphere of little games (such as catching etc) is also included for use in setting various targets and for use in different organizational forms.

2. Volume 3 "Playing and Training Creatively for the Sport of Swimming"

This trilogy of books in the "Aquafun" series is rounded off in Volume 3 with the title of "Playing and Training Creatively for the Sport of Swimming".   It covers how playing and taking part in sport in the medium of water can be made creatively and still remain fun. Chapter 1 goes into the process of how this can be effected in an educational manner.   At the beginning of each chapter of exercises, examples of an open and creative approach to this area are given (underwater diving, diving, life saving, artistic and synchronized swimming, 'aquafitness', swimming training).

These are given so that swimming instruction and training in the various facets of swimming sports can be made successful from the teaching perspective.   These are followed by many game suggestions, which could give ideas for further exercises or which can be used directly in the exercise sessions.   The fact that the process of learning a technique can be combined with games is demonstrated very clearly by the fun introduction to learning the butterfly stroke.